*The IIA Research Foundation*
*Handbook Series*

# AUDITING THE
# PROCUREMENT
# FUNCTION

By
**David O'Regan, CIA, FCA**

D1718255

**The Institute of
Internal Auditors**

**RESEARCH
FOUNDATION**
*Understanding, Guiding, Shaping*

**Disclosure**

The IIARF publishes this document for informational and educational purposes. This document is intended to provide information, but is not a substitute for legal or accounting advice. The IIARF does not provide such advice and makes no warranty as to any legal or accounting results through its publication of this document. When legal or accounting issues arise, professional assistance should be sought and retained.

The Institute of Internal Auditors' (IIA) International Professional Practices Framework for Internal Auditing (IPPF) comprises the full range of existing and developing practice guidance for the profession. The IPPF provides guidance to internal auditors globally and paves the way to world-class internal auditing.

The mission of The IIARF is to expand knowledge and understanding of internal auditing by providing relevant research and educational products to advance the profession globally.

The IIA and The IIARF work in partnership with researchers from around the globe who conduct valuable studies on critical issues affecting today's business world. Much of the content presented in their final reports is a result of IIARF-funded research and prepared as a service to The Foundation and the internal audit profession. Expressed opinions, interpretations, or points of view represent a consensus of the researchers and do not necessarily reflect or represent the official position or policies of The IIA or The IIARF.

ISBN 978-0-89413-622-1
08364   06/08
First Printing

# CONTENTS

## PART THREE – CONCLUSIONS

# ACKNOWLEDGMENTS

My primary thanks go to Erin Weber and the editorial team at The Institute of Internal Auditors Research Foundation for encouragement, perceptive criticism, and first-class project management in seeing this handbook through to publication. I also thank anonymous reviewers of the text.

I also wish to express my appreciation to several organizations and individuals for granting permission to quote from copyrighted publications. Oxford University Press gave me permission to quote from the *Oxford English Dictionary*'s definition of "procurement" in Chapter 1. Dr. John Clarke allowed me to quote in Chapter 5 from a case study in his book *Working with Monsters: How to Identify and Protect Yourself from the Workplace Psychopath* (Sydney, Australia: Random House, 2005). Also in Chapter 5, Ram Babu Nepal gave me permission to quote from his book *Development, Governance and Management* (Kathmandu, Nepal: Airawati Publication, 2007). In Chapter 10, the example of a public invitation to tender is reproduced by permission of the copyright holder, the Millennium Challenge Georgia Fund (MCG), representing the Government of Georgia.

I thank my wife, Abhishikta, for her unfailing support in this and all of my endeavors. I dedicate this book to our children, David and Abigail.

The Hague, Netherlands
February 2008

# ABOUT THE AUTHOR

**David O'Regan, CIA, FCA,** is the internal auditor of the Organization for the Prohibition of Chemical Weapons, a United Nations affiliated institution in the Netherlands. A Certified Internal Auditor and Fellow of the Institute of Chartered Accountants in England and Wales, his professional experience includes international internal auditing and financial control with United Technologies Corporation and external auditing with Price Waterhouse (forerunner to PricewaterhouseCoopers). He was also chief audit executive of Oxford University Press. He is the author of a number of books on auditing, including *Strategies for Small Audit Shops* (The IIA, 2002) and the *Auditor's Dictionary* (Wiley, 2004), and he is a contributing editor for *Internal Auditor* magazine. All views expressed in this handbook are his own.

# EXECUTIVE SUMMARY

This handbook offers practical advice for auditing the procurement function, and it is intended to be of relevance for all types and sizes of organizations throughout the world. The book is divided into three parts. In Part One, a definition of procurement as "the obtaining, through contractual agreement, of the timely and correct delivery of goods and services at best value for money" is introduced and discussed (Chapter 1). The scope of the book and the importance of procurement (the largest or second-largest category of expenditure in most organizations) are discussed (Chapter 2). The author takes the view that the core challenge of procurement is best understood in economic terms (Chapter 3), and from this starting point derives the crucial concept of "best value for money" (Chapter 4). Part One also covers the important risk areas of fraud, ethics, and socioeconomic factors (Chapters 5 and 6).

Part Two, comprising the main part of the book, addresses common risks, procedures, and internal controls at different stages of the procurement process. After summary comments (Chapter 7) and a review of procurement strategy and planning (Chapter 8), the text generally follows the typical sequence of events in the procurement cycle for individual transactions. It starts at the initiation of individual procurement actions and the selection of potential vendors, and runs through to the risk-prone and important step of the receipt and evaluation of procured goods and services. The final part of the book, Part Three, offers concluding observations, and provides and evaluates sources of further information (Chapters 15 and 16).

The author does not claim to occupy any privileged seat from which he might judge the adequacy of procurement functions. However, the author hopes to have added to the inventory of auditors' knowledge of this important topic, and that the book serves the professional interests of the auditing community.

# PART ONE
# INTRODUCTION AND
# CORE CONCEPTS

# CHAPTER 1
# DEFINING PROCUREMENT

This chapter offers a definition of procurement and explores some related terminology. It is arranged under the following headings:

- Defining Procurement
- The Definition in More Detail
- "Direct" and "Indirect" Procurement
- Other Terminology
- Procurement, Buying, and Purchasing

## Defining Procurement

Procurement is defined in this handbook as *"the obtaining, through contractual agreement, of the timely and correct delivery of goods and services at best value for money."* This definition has several important components (which are discussed in turn below), but it is first worth noting that there is no universally agreed definition of procurement. However, although a number of other definitions are in circulation, they tend to be little more than variations of the definition given here. For example, the *Oxford English Dictionary* offers two definitions of procurement: (1) a brief definition as "the action or process of obtaining supplies and equipment," and (2) one that is closer to the definition used in this book — "the acquisition of goods and services at the best possible price, in appropriate quantities, at the right time and place, etc."[1]

---

[1] Available from the *Oxford English Dictionary* online (www.oed.com) November 2007. This dictionary entry records that the word "procurement" entered English in the 13th century through Anglo-Norman French, and that its contemporary organizational meaning (as used in this book) originates from military usage.

## The Definition in More Detail

Having defined procurement as *"the obtaining, through contractual agreement, of the timely and correct delivery of goods and services at best value for money,"* we may look further into individual aspects of the definition. We should emphasize that procurement involves the "obtaining through contractual agreement" of goods and services, which stresses the formal, legal nature of procurement. We are not considering informal mechanisms of obtaining goods and services, but rather a series of organizational procedures and arrangements whose outcome is underpinned by explicit legal commitments. (Contractual and wider legal matters are examined in more depth in Chapter 13.)

Our definition refers to both "goods and services" as it intends to capture the procurement of all tangible and intangible items, ranging from physical assets like computer hardware to services like office cleaning. The use of the phrase "goods and services" is to be understood in the widest possible sense.

The definition also refers to the "timely and correct delivery" of goods and services, as a procured good or service must be satisfactorily delivered or performed in the appropriate location for a procurement action to meet its objectives. The timeliness of procurement delivery is also central to organizational interests. (In Chapter 14, issues arising in the area of the receipt and evaluation of procured goods and services are considered.)

The final element of the definition that we shall consider is the phrase "best value for money." This refers to the optimal balance between obtaining a sufficient quantity and quality of goods and services on one hand, and minimizing the total cost of these goods and services on the other. When we talk of "total costs," we are describing not merely the vendor's selling prices as formalized in a contractual agreement, but all related costs arising from a procurement action, including inventory storage and even reputation costs. (The economic aspects of procurement are explored further in Chapter 3, and Chapter 4 covers the concept of "best value for money.")

## "Direct" and "Indirect" Procurement

A further refinement of the definition of procurement can be seen in the frequently encountered terms "direct procurement" and "indirect procurement." Although they are not developed further in this handbook, they are discussed here for completeness. In a manufacturing context, direct procurement relates to procurement specifically for production processes, typically covering raw materials and other direct elements of manufacturing. In contrast, indirect production refers to procurement that is not specifically related to production, such as operating and overhead costs like spare parts, office supplies, and clerical services.[2]

A less frequent use of the terms "direct procurement" and "indirect procurement" is to distinguish, respectively, between a procurement process that engages directly with the vendor of a good or service procured and a procurement process that may use an intermediary, such as an agent or an outsourcer. The rest of this handbook does not make reference to any distinctions between direct and indirect procurement.

---

[2]It is worth noting that "direct procurement" defined in this manner is a major component in supply chain management (SCM). SCM may be understood as a cross-functional approach to planning, controlling, and coordinating elements of manufacturing and conversion processes that encourages the highest possible economy, efficiency, and effectiveness, and the meeting of customer expectations. SCM typically encompasses all steps in the process of inventory movements and storage, from materials requirements planning through the sourcing of raw materials to the point of consumption of finished goods. Procurement is only one aspect of SCM.

## Other Terminology

The field of procurement has a large number of specialist terms, and this jargon often varies slightly from organization to organization. For purposes of consistency, we settled on one term for use throughout the text, but the glossary at the end of the book summarizes some common alternatives. For example, "requisition for procurement" is sometimes used as an alternative for the term "request for procurement." (The latter is used in this book.) In both these cases, the acronym RFP is the same.

In addition, we use the term "official" to refer to an organizational employee with a defined function. Examples are "procurement official" and "legal official."

## Procurement, Buying, and Purchasing

The terms "buying" and "purchasing" are often used synonymously with "procurement." This is best avoided, in the author's view, on the grounds that buying and purchasing may be seen as subsets of the wider procurement function. Buying and purchasing may suggest a focus on the earlier stages of the procurement process that involve the handling of requests for procurement, the selection of vendors through quotations or tendering processes, the issuance of purchase orders, and possibly also assistance in contractual negotiations with vendors. These processes may not cover the later stages of a procurement action, like the verification of the accurate and timely receipt of a good or service. Therefore, we do not treat these terms interchangeably, although in practice this may be encountered.

# CHAPTER 2
# THE SCOPE OF
# THE HANDBOOK

This chapter summarizes the scope of this handbook's contents and is arranged under the following headings:

- What This Handbook Covers
- What This Handbook Does Not Cover

## What This Handbook Covers

In this handbook, the author sets out the basic principles, practices, risks, and internal controls of procurement that are likely to be of most interest to auditors. The focus is on areas of universal interest in procurement, and the author has attempted to steer the handbook into practical directions, avoiding any emphasis on abstract theory. He hopes to have pruned the topic down to its core essentials, compressing the content as far as is compatible with intelligibility and usefulness.

The potential readership of this handbook is wide. The author has sought to provide adequate information for all auditors, while in Chapter 16 there is guidance for further sources of specialized information. The handbook does not make any assumptions about the nature of the auditing circumstances of the reader — it is aimed at internal auditors, external auditors, and all those with an interest in the field of the auditing of procurement (including members of audit committees, procurement professionals, and those who are subject to auditing). Nonetheless, despite this intention for the widest possible readership, this handbook was written with the express intention of ensuring consistency with the _International Standards for the Professional Practice of Internal Auditing_ and the International Professional Practices Framework of The Institute of Internal Auditors.

Further, the author makes no assumptions about the institutional, cultural, or geographical context in which the auditing of procurement takes place. The handbook aims to cover the essentials of procurement that are of practical relevance around the world, in the private sector, the not-for-profit or charitable sectors, local and national government, and international organizations. To underline the global applicability of the concepts in this book, examples of procurement-related considerations have been taken from countries as varied as Australia, Georgia, and Nepal.

The handbook does not make any assumptions about the degree of manual or automated administrative and accounting systems in the reader's organization, or the size of the organization and the materiality of its procurement function — other than the assumption that the procurement function is of sufficient materiality to warrant the attention of auditors. In some organizations, procurement is a major function that accounts for a high proportion of expenditure. In other organizations it may be more modest, albeit still important. Some auditors are dedicated specifically to auditing procurement functions, while in other cases the procurement function may be part of an audit universe that competes with other topics for the auditor's attention.

The author sought to make the handbook valid for any methods by which the reader's organization delegates its rights to authorize transactions, for any disbursement mechanisms that an organization may use (like functional or departmental credit cards for smaller items of procurement), and for any risk management practices.

It is, of course, natural to recognize that individual organizations are likely to have particular circumstances that affect the manner in which they undertake procurement. For example, in the United States the record-keeping requirements of the Foreign Corrupt Practices Act of 1977 may have a major impact on an organization's procurement activity. However, this handbook consciously focuses on matters of global applicability and gives case studies and examples of procurement activity from around the world.

The author offers an additional comment on the contents of this handbook. Among the discussions of risks and internal controls in this text, examples are given of procurement fraud. Some readers may be uncomfortable with the inclusion of such material in the sense that it may plant suggestions in unethical minds. To this the author would respond that the information in this handbook is intended to assist in safeguarding against such activities and thereby offer enhanced protection against frequently under-recognized procurement risks. In the author's view, it is better for the auditor to approach procurement with this information in mind than to be at the mercy of poor internal controls or the bad intentions of unscrupulous individuals.

## What This Handbook Does Not Cover

This handbook focuses directly on procurement rather than on the expenditure cycle as a whole. Therefore, it does not address in detail several topics related to expenditure on goods and services — budgeting processes; accounts payable and general ledger practices; accounting for fixed assets; disbursement mechanisms; logistics; foreign currency exchange; inventory systems; and contracts with consultants. All these are important elements of the expenditure cycle and its related activities, and they merit the auditor's attention. However, the handbook only mentions them in passing, and to the extent that they relate to the core topic of procurement.

Specialist areas of procurement, like e-procurement (electronic procurement), electronic data interchange, and just-in-time systems (that aim to minimize inventory holdings), are briefly mentioned in the text, but a generalist, modestly sized book of this nature cannot treat these specialized topics in depth. Finally, the handbook only mentions in passing very minor purchases that might normally be paid out of petty cash in most organizations, and minor travel-related incidentals (like taxi fares).

# CHAPTER 3
# THE CORE
# ECONOMIC CHALLENGE
# OF PROCUREMENT

In this handbook we consider a wide spectrum of procurement matters of interest to auditors, including financial, legal, and ethical considerations. There is much complexity in all these areas. However, it is the author's view that economic activity is at the core of procurement and the other considerations either derive from or challenge this economic foundation. An understanding of the core economic challenge of procurement can therefore assist in clarifying the matters at stake and give the auditor a handle on the types of complexity that we shall meet later in the book. This chapter is arranged under the following headings:

- Economics and Scarcity
- Alternative Uses of Resources
- Competition
- Marginality and Other Economic Concepts
- Constraints on Procurement as a Classic Economic Activity

## Economics and Scarcity

The classical view of the main task of economics is the allocation of scarce resources that have alternative uses. This concept of economics stresses the importance of scarcity. In a Utopian setting like the Garden of Eden, there may be systems for the production and distribution of goods and services, but this is not an economy as we would understand it, as everything is available in unlimited quantities. There was no scarcity in the Garden of Eden and no need to economize.

This concept of economics serves our purposes in this book, as procurement is essentially a means of obtaining goods and services by using scarce resources. Owing to the financial constraints that face any organization, it is not feasible to undertake unlimited procurement. An organization is forced into choices on how to spend its resources — it must make decisions, make sacrifices, and economize. This concept of scarcity is relatively intuitive and easily grasped, and it is a key element underpinning the notion of "best value for money" that we shall discuss further in Chapter 4. However, other considerations of greater and lesser complexity flow from the economic concept of alternative uses, and we shall discuss these in the remainder of this chapter.

## Alternative Uses of Resources

In the context of procurement, "alternative uses" refers to the goods and services that an organization could acquire were it to forego other available goods and services. Or, to put it another way, it is the cost of not doing something else (sometimes known as an opportunity cost).

If one dollar had only one use, things would be simple. But every dollar spent by an organization on a good or service is a dollar that could have been spent on another good or service — or not spent at all and invested in a bank account. Deciding on how to maximize the benefits to an organization from spending (or not spending) money is not always easy to define. Choices and trade-offs are the stuff of economics, and of procurement. The scarcity and alternative uses of resources combine to make the task of the procurement function a challenging one.

## Competition

In classical views of economics, price mechanisms operate to ensure the optimal matching of the demand and supply of goods and services, and competitive pressures underpin these price mechanisms. If a large number of buyers and sellers rival one another, the resulting strong competition normally encourages downward pressures on prices. Using this logic, a basic principle of procurement is the maximization of competition among potential vendors of goods and services. A competitive element should therefore be evident in the fabric of a procurement function's activities to ensure that it focuses on the optimal use of the organization's resources. (The role of competition in procurement is discussed in more detail in Chapter 11.)

### Marginality and Other Economic Concepts

In classical economic theory, resources are allocated in the most optimal way when prices are equal to the additional cost of producing one more unit of a good or service. This is often known as the "marginal cost." For our purposes, there is no need to go into the complexities of marginal analysis, but we may note that economic decisions are often made on the basis of their marginal impact. In terms of procurement, decisions on the use of an organization's funds that are earmarked for procurement can have a significant, incremental impact on the organization. The margins of decision making can be extremely sensitive for an organization's cost base.

Two other economic concepts may be mentioned here. The "law of diminishing returns" suggests that, beyond a certain point, the value of additional units of a good or service decreases at an escalating rate. Some economists reject the validity of the law of diminishing returns in favor of "indifference curves," which attempt to measure economic preferences between alternatives. Both concepts are of potential relevance to procurement in the sense that they suggest that at some point of expenditure on a good or service, a potential alternative use of the expenditure becomes more prominent.

We do not need to enter into the technicalities of these concepts, but we should be aware of their implications for procurement. For example, for each individual procurement action there may be a point at which procurement becomes "over-procurement" and therefore counterproductive and against the best interests of the organization.

## Constraints on Procurement as a Classic Economic Activity

So far in this chapter, we have suggested that the classical concept of economics as the allocation of scarce resources that have alternative uses is a valuable foundation for understanding the core challenges of procurement. In our discussion of the economic context of procurement, the assumptions have been those of classical (or neoclassical) economics, in which prices are established through the free interaction of supply and demand in competitive market conditions, without restrictions on the distribution of goods and services and in which no economic factors can significantly distort the market. Under such conditions, information flows are available to all participants in the market, and there is freedom of entry to and exit from the market.

Of course, in the real world, there are many constraints on the operations of markets. At one extreme is the command economy with centralized economic planning by the government, which, in the "liberalized" early 21st century, is restricted to a relatively small number of countries in the world. For example, at the time of this writing, a procurement function operating in a country like North Korea or Cuba would have its economic options severely constrained by state economic planning requirements.

Even in more liberal economic environments, constraints to competitive markets can derive from government planning on a lesser but still meaningful scale. In addition, legislation, lobbying groups, public opinion, subsidies, economic sanctions, and other factors can influence a market for goods and services. For example, a government procurement function in a specific country may be instructed — for political reasons of protectionism or national security — to purchase only items manufactured in that specific country or a politically allied country. To take another example, oil prices are influenced by the political and economic decisions of the Organization of the Petroleum Exporting Countries (OPEC), an Austrian-based international organization that sets oil production targets for its members.

However, despite the real-world imperfections of the economic model outlined in this chapter, the author suggests that procurement can be best understood through a consideration of its economic foundations — the allocation of limited resources (i.e., procurement funds) that have alternative uses; the use of prices to determine the basic costs (but not the "full costs") of procurement activity; the importance of a competitive basis for procurement activity; and the marginal impact of procurement decision making.[3]

---

[3]This chapter's brief summary of economic principles cannot, of course, give anything like an adequate account of the complexity of the subject. Succinct definitions of a range of economic concepts (including classical economics, neoclassical economics, indifference curves, marginalism, and the command economy) are available in Roger Scruton, *Dictionary of Political Thought* (New York, NY: Palgrave Macmillan, revised edition, 2007).

# CHAPTER 4
# BEST VALUE FOR MONEY

In the previous chapter we reviewed the core economic principles of procurement.  In this chapter we develop these foundational concepts to consider a crucial element of our definition of procurement as "the obtaining, through contractual agreement, of the timely and correct delivery of goods and services *at best value for money*" (emphasis added).

A reckless input of funds to a procurement function without due consideration of the outcomes would serve no positive end for an organization.  When a procurement function decides on the best value for money offered by alternative courses of action, it must weigh the costs and benefits of each potential action.  Obtaining "best value for money" (sometimes referred to as the "best price/quality ratio" and the "most economically advantageous" course of action) entails a search for the optimal balance between maximizing the quantity and quality of goods and services on one hand, and minimizing the total cost of these goods and services on the other.

In the case of the procurement of a good whose characteristics are indistinguishable between those offered by a number of potential vendors (or at least whose characteristics vary little, as with a commodity like oil), the choice often boils down to a decision on price.  However, even in a simple procurement action of this type, there may be other important factors to consider, including delivery schedules, storage arrangements, and the reliability of supply, any of which may vary significantly between potential vendors.

Performing a cost/benefit analysis for goods or services that have more complex technical specifications is a significant challenge.  In such a context, it is not simply a case of procuring the cheapest good or service on the market, while ensuring reliable supply or storage arrangements. The procurement function may need to weigh a wide range of considerations. For example, how much quality of a good or service can be sacrificed, or "traded off," in order to secure a lower price? Procurement functions approach these matters through technical and economic evaluations (see Chapter 12).

To take one side of the cost/benefit equation, the determination of the total cost of a procurement action is often tricky. The starting point is clearly the contractually agreed price that will be concluded with a vendor. In addition to this, other costs need to be captured by the decision-making process, from expenditure on inventory storage and in-house administrative work that are relatively straightforward to quantify, to more qualitative costs like reputation costs. Further, all costs and benefits must be weighed over the entire life of the procurement cycle and, if necessary, even beyond. The disposal costs of equipment and longer-term environmental costs are good examples of longer-term considerations.

In summary, a comprehensive assessment of costs and benefits should be made for all major procurement actions, with the overriding concern that the procurement action must be in the interests of the organization. Establishing the point at which the cost/benefit trade-off is optimized is the core challenge of procurement. And it is a significant challenge.

# CHAPTER 5
# PROCUREMENT AND FRAUD

In Part Two of this handbook we look at specific risks at various stages of the procurement process. Before proceeding into the details of procedural risks in Part Two, it is appropriate to stand back and take stock of the larger picture. Several broad risk categories — fraud (discussed in this chapter), ethics, terrorism, and socioeconomic issues (discussed in the following chapter) — influence many of the specific risks discussed later in the handbook. This chapter is arranged under the following headings:

- What is Fraud?
- A Case Study of Fraud
- Who Commits Fraud – and Why?
- What Fraud Isn't

## What is Fraud?

Fraud is illegal, dishonest, or improper activity that includes the theft of assets and the manipulation of accounting data and sensitive information. Procurement is often vulnerable to fraud, and it can involve material amounts. Quite simply, in many organizations, procurement is where the money is. Procurement fraud can inflict immense economic damage on an organization; in extreme cases it might even destabilize and bring down an organization.

Procurement functions tend to be located at the center of a network of significant communication flows of a price-sensitive nature, both within an organization and between an organization and external parties, and it can offer scope for the making of personal gains from procurement actions. From behind a facade of organizational loyalty, a determined and predatory fraudster can detect vulnerable points in a procurement system while hiding, chameleon-like, in the fabric of an organization. A fraudster typically exploits weak points in a procurement system, whether he or she is opportunistic or systematic, and whether acting alone or in collusion with outside parties. For this reason, the specific internal controls set out in Part Two are vitally important to minimize the risks of fraud.

In preceding chapters we emphasized the economic aspects of procurement. The topic of fraud can also be viewed through an economic lens, in that fraudulent activity may be interpreted as attempts to subvert the smooth economic operation of procurement actions. For example, fraud may corrupt the competitive element of the procurement process through favoritism to specific potential vendors, thereby undermining the objective of obtaining best value for money.

A crucial risk minimization tool in this area is the recognition of potential conflicts of interest among an organization's employees who are involved in procurement. A conflict of interest arises when there is an incompatibility between rights and responsibilities that can give rise to an employee receiving a direct or indirect benefit from a procurement action. Essentially, the conflict is one between the best interests of the organization on one hand, and the best private interests of an employee on the other. The existence of a conflict of interest tends to make it difficult for an employee to deal with an outside party on a fully objective, arm's length basis.

A conflict of interest may arise when an employee involved in a procurement action has an economic, family, or emotional interest in a potential vendor (through stock ownership; the acceptance of gifts, fees, commissions, or bribes; or family connections to a vendor). In such circumstances, the employee's impartiality is inevitably compromised. As a result, even if the employee strives to act with the highest objectivity, there is at a minimum a *perception* of improper influence over the manner in which he or she handles a procurement action. Needless to say, an employee with a conflict of interest should not participate in a procurement process that may be affected by that conflict of interest. If an organization permits an employee to participate in a procurement action under such circumstances, the employee should declare the conflict of interest through the organization's predetermined reporting channels.

However, it is not only among employees of an organization, or between employees and potential vendors, that fraud can occur. It can also originate among potential vendors without the knowledge of the organization's employees. For example, collusion among two or more potential vendors may aim at fixing prices at higher levels than would be the case under fully competitive conditions. It may be extremely difficult for an organization's procurement function to detect anticompetitive, vendor bidding rings. However, when such activity is known, the vendors involved should be excluded from doing future business with the organization until such time as the organization is satisfied that new ethical principles have been established by the vendors (for example, through a change of management).

In serious cases, external authorities may need to be informed of fraudulent activity and price-fixing cartels. The nature of the external authorities varies around the world, but it should be noted that many countries have anticorruption bodies that monitor corruption in public life, and this includes procurement-related corruption. To take an example from South Asia, "the Commission for the Investigation of Abuse of Authority (CIAA) is the central anti-corruption authority of Nepal...involved in conducting inquiries and investigations against improper conduct and corruption committed by a person holding public office...and filing a case before the court of law."[4]

---

[4]Ram Babu Nepal, *Development, Governance and Management* (Kathmandu, Nepal: Airawati Publication, 2007), 241.

In summary, procurement fraud is corrupt, parasitic behavior that feeds off and diminishes the procurement process, thereby causing economic damage to an organization. The "disease" of fraudulent activity is often intertwined with the "healthy tissue" of an organization, enhancing its danger and making its identification and eradication difficult. The auditor should plan audit work in line with the level of the risk of fraud in a specific organization. For example, lax management practices and poor internal controls tend to increase the risks of procurement fraud. In Chapter 14, which deals with the receipt and evaluation of procured goods and services, we discuss a range of procedures and internal controls that can minimize the risks of fraud.

## A Case Study of Fraud

The following case study of fraud is from Australia[5] and in it the name has been changed for confidentiality purposes:

> "Jeff was a twenty-four-year-old accountant in a large marketing firm. He was frustrated that the company could not see his potential for doing more important work rather than processing payments. He also believed he was underpaid... Jeff decided he would teach the company a lesson and make some money for himself at the same time. He set up a 'shelf company.' He then designed an exclusive-looking letterhead for a general sounding company and rented a post office box for all correspondence. He wrote a bill to the company he was working for, from his 'shelf company,' charging them for services that had never been rendered. One of Jeff's responsibilities was to process

---

[5]John Clarke, *Working With Monsters: How to Identify and Protect Yourself from the Workplace Psychopath* (Sydney, Australia: Random House, 2005), 111-112.

incoming bills... He would process his own bill, write out a check, and hand it to the senior accountant. The bill was paid without question.

"He continued doing this until he was finally caught when a company auditor tried to contact Jeff's 'shelf company' and found that it was false. When the police fraud squad investigated, they discovered that the bank accounts linked to the shelf company belonged to Jeff. For over six months, Jeff had fraudulently obtained approximately $100,000. Only $4,000 was recovered from his bank account."

In reading this example of an Australian fraud, the reader may sense the drone of a distant didjeridoo — like that instrument, the circumstances of the case study may seem far away and exotic. Yet the author chose this specific case study because it is a fairly typical example of an organizational fraud, and it raises a number of interesting questions about procurement risks and internal controls. It points to the importance of the maintenance by the procurement function of a roster of vendors that the procurement function alone can amend (discussed further in Chapter 10); the need for a suitable segregation of responsibilities between the accounting and procurement functions (Chapters 8 and 10); and the requirement for a credible process for receiving and evaluating goods and services before payment is made (Chapter 14). (The case study does not specify the sizes of the individual transactions involved, but it raises questions about competition-related procurement thresholds, as discussed in Chapter 11.)

## Who Commits Fraud – and Why?

We drew attention earlier in this chapter to the risks of fraudsters hiding, chameleon-like, in the fabric of an organization. A fraudster may be an employee in a procurement function who has access to sensitive or confidential information, or an employee of another organizational function who may try to bamboozle inexperienced procurement function employees (especially in the technical evaluation stage of the procurement process, as discussed in Chapter 12).

It is difficult for the auditor to fathom fully the motivations that underpin fraudulent behavior and that may present warning signs. A range of possible contextual pressures may lead to procurement fraud. For example, it is sometimes suggested that procurement fraud is driven by extreme poverty, although procurement fraud (and white-collar crime generally) seems in general to be committed by intelligent, middle-class individuals who are already affluent but crave further wealth and social status.

In addition to pure greed, there are many other possible motivations for procurement fraud. For example, victims of blackmail may feel a desperate need to raise cash. Fraud may also be motivated by the financing of an addiction to gambling or drugs, or to meet the expensive tastes of a secret lover. As we saw in our Australian case study, a disgruntled employee may seek to "get back" at an employer. In other cases, fraud may simply appeal to "thrill seekers" whose need for excitement is achieved by breaking organizational rules.

The wide range of possible motivations for fraud makes it difficult for the auditor to attempt to recognize warning signs of potential procurement fraud. One sometimes hears of behavioral "indicators" of fraud, like an individual who lives a luxurious lifestyle above his or her apparent spending power, or who refuses to take vacations in order to keep a tight control over their area of work. These warning signs may be valid indicators of fraud risk, but they offer dangerous foundations for an auditor to leap to assumptions of fraudulent activity. For example, an employee on a modest salary may be able to live a luxurious lifestyle as a result of receiving cash from other, legitimate sources, like an inheritance. And an employee who takes few vacations may be a workaholic rather than a fraudster.

In conclusion, when it comes to trying to preempt fraudulent behavior, there are no hard-and-fast rules. The best the auditor can do is to assume that any weaknesses in the procurement system run the risk of being exploited, and that such weaknesses should be minimized by appropriate procedures and internal controls.

## What Fraud Isn't

The failure to obtain best value for money in a procurement process is, of course, not always due to fraud. This is because fraud requires deceitful intentions. Procurement problems may arise from unintentional errors and from "innocent" deviations from internal controls. For example, inadequate technical evaluations in a procurement exercise might lead to the acquisition of unnecessarily expensive goods or services.

Although the intention to defraud an organization is absent in such cases, the impact of negligence and carelessness can be as great as that arising from fraudulent activity. The procedures and internal controls discussed in Part Two illustrate areas in which unintentional errors may prove disastrous for the organization. First, however, we shall look in Chapter 6 at another broad set of procurement risks.

# CHAPTER 6
# ETHICS AND
# SOCIOECONOMIC ISSUES

In the preceding chapters, we focused on the economic aspects of procurement, with an emphasis on matters like cost/benefit analyses, the importance of competition, and the risks of attempts to subvert the economic process through fraud. In this chapter, we shall consider factors that are not primarily economic.

In many countries today, best practices in organizational governance require organizations to attempt to integrate economic considerations with ethical, environmental, and social considerations. This chapter is arranged under the following headings:

- Ethics in Practice
- Terrorism and Organized Crime
- Sustainability and Socioeconomic Issues
- Stakeholders and Reputation Risk

## Ethics in Practice

The subject of ethics is a massive and complex one, and space permits only a brief summary here. Among the sources of ethics — which may be understood as the application of consistent moral judgment to achieve responsible, honest conduct — are religion, secular and humanistic traditions, systems of law, customs, and folk wisdom. Given the wide variety of ethical sources, it is not surprising that there may be conflicting views of the legitimacy of specific ethical matters. However, in the area of procurement, in practice it seems to be relatively straightforward to determine what is ethical and what is not. This straightforwardness is even evident in international contexts, despite cultural differences.

It has been suggested that although "there is not always a unanimous opinion about what is ethical and what is not...*the question must generally be settled by a decision* as to what is right and what is wrong."[6] In other words, an ethical basis for procurement can be established by organizational decisions, usually expressed in a formal ethical procurement policy or code of conduct that addresses the core theme of serving the best interests of the organization and limiting the scope for improper activities.

Any statement of ethics should be as specific as possible. For example, it is of limited value to forbid gifts or hospitality of low materiality, as the definition of "low materiality" is open to interpretation. It is generally preferable to state a monetary limit on permitted gifts or hospitality (say, of $20), or even to forbid outright any hospitality or gifts, irrespective of value. (The latter course of action may be difficult, as social and cultural practices in some contexts may make a blanket ban impractical.) In general, an ethical procurement policy must be unambiguous and precise in order to provide a firm administrative basis for ethical practices.

The formalization of an ethical procurement policy or code of conduct is a first step. Equally important is the communication of the policy to employees (and even third parties). The avoidance of excessively legalistic jargon can enhance the understandability of the document, which should be published and disseminated widely through appropriate organizational channels (including Web sites).

---

[6]Mortimer A. Dittenhofer and Douglas E. Ziegenfuss, *Ethics and the Internal Auditor: 20 Years Later* (Altamonte Springs, FL: The Institute of Internal Auditors, 2004), 1 and 4. Emphasis added.

Employee training courses on ethics can also support the ethical foundation of procurement. Also, acceptance of the ethical policy can be made a condition of employment in an organization's procurement function.

## Terrorism and Organized Crime

These are troubling times for the ethical and social conscience, and no area is of more concern in the unstable, globalized world of the early 21st century than that of political and religious violence and of organized crime (in areas like people trafficking). These matters are primarily the responsibility of governmental and international law enforcement institutions. However, all organizations that disburse funds through procurement mechanisms have a role to play in this arena, as organizations should try to avoid giving any assistance to criminals or terrorists. This is sometimes easier said than done.

At a minimum, organizations should implement reasonable safeguards against the subsequent use of funds that they have disbursed to finance terrorism and crime. The consequences of not taking adequate safeguards can lead to suffering and death and cause extreme damage to an organization's credibility. Specific antiterrorism procurement provisions of this nature include being aware of organizations and governments identified by credible authorities as having links with terrorism. More generally, the importance of the selection and evaluations of vendors is central to this topic. Chapter 10 reviews fundamental internal controls in this area.

## Sustainability and Socioeconomic Issues

Sustainability — the pursuit of economic activity without excessive degradation of the physical and social environment — is central to good organizational citizenship. It requires organizations and their procurement functions to balance economic considerations with sustainable values, respect for human rights, the treatment of minorities, and gender equality.

There are many potential conflicts between economic and non-economic factors, and this vast topic can only be touched on lightly in this handbook. It should be emphasized that we are not necessarily talking about a full-fledged "green procurement" or "ethical procurement" but rather a suitable balancing of economic and non-economic factors. Again, as with ethics, it is advisable for an organization to have policies in place in relation to these matters. In terms of procurement, these policies may be included in a vendor code of conduct, or they may form part of the organization's standard terms and conditions.

## Stakeholders and Reputation Risk

Modern organizational stakeholder theory casts a wide net in its identification of stakeholders. The "traditional" stakeholders of investors, employees, and tax authorities are now generally assumed to be supplemented by a range of individuals and organizations with an interest in an organization's activities. Most organizations' networks of rights and responsibilities seem to stretch ever wider. For example, the stakeholders of a manufacturing organization may be considered to include the local residents who live near production facilities; its customers; its vendors; and the wider public (who may follow the organization's activities in the media).

An organization's reputation rests on its stakeholders' perceptions, as defined in the widest sense. For all the categories of risk discussed in this and the preceding chapter, an organization's reputation can be eroded or shattered in the court of public opinion. A serious fraud, unethical practices, alleged links to terrorism, and indeed any flouting of stakeholder concerns can dent an organization's social and even political standing. Reputation risk is very real, and from it serious consequences may flow, ranging from political interference to stakeholder activism, protests, and boycotts. Commercial organizations may experience a decline in the value of their stocks and exclusion from some "ethically oriented" investment vehicles. Therefore, however contested this subject may be, most organizations cannot ignore their stakeholders' perceptions, even if they wished to do so.

An example of the ramifications of reputation risk can be seen (at the time of this writing, in late 2007) with the recall on safety grounds of Chinese-made children's toys by a number of corporations in the United States, the United Kingdom, and Australia. Manufacturing defects that led to the product recalls were attributed by some observers to the subcontracting of manufacturing processes to Chinese vendors who failed to follow agreed safety norms, though the balance of responsibility between Chinese manufacturing quality and western design matters remained unclear. Child safety is an issue that tends to generate strong emotions, and the resulting reputation damage affected not only the corporations themselves and their vendors, but also the Chinese economy itself, as anxious Chinese politicians sought to reassure world markets of the reliability of the country's manufacturing processes. This example shows how procurement-related reputation risk can have immense organizational and political ramifications.

On a more positive note, the conduct of competitive tendering (as discussed in Chapter 11) can bolster an organization's reputation to the extent that it plays a role in establishing an organization's name for fair dealings and transparency.

# PART TWO
# THE PROCUREMENT PROCESS:
# PROCEDURES AND
# INTERNAL CONTROLS

# CHAPTER 7
# AUDITING BASIC
# PROCEDURES AND
# INTERNAL CONTROLS

In Part Two of the handbook, we shall move from broad themes to specific aspects of the procurement process. It is important that an organization has clear and verifiable procurement procedures in place, in which are embedded preventative internal controls that are intended to anticipate any problems that may weaken the procurement process. Recurring themes in Part Two include competition, transparency, objectivity, confidentiality, fairness, and efficiency. We saw the overall contours of these and similar concerns in Part One. Now it's time to look at the specific checks and balances in the procurement process.

In order to audit the procurement process, it is important for the auditor to have a good understanding of the process' details rather than to focus merely on its inputs and outputs. One cannot simply sidestep the details of procurement activity. To give an analogy, one can envision a purported mechanic who knows how to change a car's tires, wash its windows, polish its bodywork, fill it with gas, and bash out any dents, but who has little understanding of the engine. Such a mechanic would send any car that doesn't work to the scrap yard. No one would consider this mechanic to be competent. Similarly, the auditor must know what happens "under the hood" of an organization's operations; in other words, how the mechanics of the procurement process work, and what to look for during an audit.

The author has made no assumptions about the specific institutional arrangements that may affect an organization's procurement systems, processes, and controls. For example, it does not assume that the organization has a fully centralized procurement function, nor a decentralized one. Instead, the author has attempted to focus on important elements common to most procurement processes, without attempting to fit them into any presupposed institutional framework. These elements include high-level procurement strategy and planning, and various steps in the procurement process for individual procurement actions, from the request for procurement through the delivery and evaluation of goods and services.

The approach has been to highlight key elements of a sound procurement function, and by default the absence or incompleteness of any of the elements covered in the following chapters give rise to risks and potential internal control weaknesses. Each chapter includes a summary of important procedural risks and finishes with a summary of major audit implications of the points raised in the chapter.

A final note of caution: Individual organizations may have legitimate reasons for variances from the patterns discussed in the following chapters. What follows are not mechanical rules, but rather core considerations that the auditor of a procurement function should consider in the course of his or her work.

# CHAPTER 8
# PROCUREMENT STRATEGY AND PLANNING

Before we consider procedures and controls over individual procurement transactions, it must be emphasized that an adequate organization-wide procurement strategy and related planning process are necessary to manage the acquisition of goods and services. A detailed procurement plan should derive from a high-level procurement strategy, which in turn should be consistent with the organization's overall objectives. The procurement plan should take the form of a schedule of procurement activity, analyzed at the level of individual procurement actions, which is as accurate as possible in terms of costs and timelines, and which is updated frequently. This chapter is arranged under the following headings:

- Procurement Strategy
- Procurement Planning
- Procedural Considerations and Risks
- Audit Implications

## Procurement Strategy

An organization's procurement strategy is a high-level policy or set of policies that ensures that procurement activity is framed within the organization's wider objectives. It addresses topics like the nature of the required procurement activity, the frequency of procurement actions, and the methodology for ensuring adequate competition. The auditor should ascertain and understand the nature of the organization's procurement strategy, and conduct audits in light of the strategy.

We shall consider three areas that most organizational procurement strategies tend to address. The first is a tension between short-term and long-term procurement objectives. Short-term, frequent procurement actions encourage competitive prices for procured goods and services. However, very frequent solicitations of procurement actions may result in high short-term costs (like administrative costs) that result from the frequent switching between vendors, and also in harmful longer-term consequences of damage to the stability of an organization's relationships with vendors.

A second important and common focus of procurement strategy concerns the size of procurement actions. Should an organization undertake individual procurement actions for major slices of activity, or rather divide large areas of procurement into smaller "lots" for individual, competitive procurement actions? Here, there is an obvious tension between achieving economies of scale through a smaller number of procurement actions on one hand, and encouraging low costs through intensive price competition on the other. (Also, a large number of small procurement actions may lower the risks of vendor collusion, owing to the difficulties of arranging collusion among a large number of participating, potential vendors.)

A third area of procurement strategy is the need to define the relative importance of economic and non-economic factors. In Chapter 6 we reviewed socioeconomic and sustainability considerations. An organization's procurement strategy should set a framework for resolving the tensions between purely economic and wider socioeconomic factors. For example, an organization may wish to obtain some of its goods from organizations that stress environmentally friendly activities, even though these goods may exceed typical market costs.

It is also worth mentioning that an organization's procurement strategy should be consistent with its strategies in other functions and operational areas. For example, a manufacturing organization that aims to minimize inventory holdings through the use of a just-in-time system of inventory delivery must reflect its inventory management strategy in its procurement strategy (and in related areas like production planning).

In summary, it is difficult to exaggerate the importance of a procurement strategy that is congruent with the organization's wider strategic objectives, and which drives individual procurement actions. With a procurement strategy that hits the metaphorical tuning fork, all the organization's procurement plans and actions should start vibrating in harmony, thereby minimizing risks.

## Procurement Planning

Adequate procurement planning is necessary to ensure that individual procurement actions are initiated in sufficient time to meet operational needs. This should assist in avoiding last-minute transactions in which important elements of the procurement process (like the careful selection of vendors on the basis of market research, or fully competitive tendering) are undertaken hurriedly, or even sidestepped altogether. Adequate procurement planning should also ensure that a procurement function is not overstretched by compressing too much activity into a short time frame: it should be linked to an assessment of procurement function staffing requirements.

Procurement planning typically starts from a statement of the organization's procurement strategy and develops into a detailed schedule of the entire organization's anticipated procurement activity. The sources of information for procurement inputs into the organization include the organization's budgets; operating plans; input from individual functions on their expenditure intentions; and a schedule of expiring, existing procurement agreements.

The procurement function should prepare a procurement needs (or requirements) assessment that covers the overall requirements of the organization, and should break down the analysis into individual procurement actions. The assessment should have cost estimates and time scales for individual procurement actions to allow for a review of the adequacy of funding and the consistency of the procurement plan with the timings of expected cash flows. This procurement assessment should identify potential economies of scale. To ensure its continuing validity as a useful management tool, the plan requires regular updating (typically monthly or quarterly).

Normally, one would expect the organization's top management to determine procurement strategy, and the procurement function to be responsible for the preparation and implementation of the detailed procurement plan. Appropriate input from other parts of the organization is normally necessary to create a valid procurement plan. In some cases, the procurement function's role in the preparation of the organizational procurement plan may be focused on the consolidation of procurement plans prepared by various units in the organization. In most cases, however, the procurement function is likely to take the lead role in procurement planning. Whatever the particular circumstances, a clear framework for the responsibility and accountability of the procurement function is essential. This typically includes the identification of responsible organizational units and officials for each procurement action, with details of any cross-functional procurement actions that require coordination between two or more parts of the organization.

The time period covered by a procurement plan is normally for the following 12 or 24 months. However, the procurement plan may be significantly longer in cases when long-term operational considerations are important. Examples of this include capital projects that spread over a number of years.

Owing to its importance, the procurement plan should be approved at an appropriate level of the organization — normally by an official from the organization's "top table," and perhaps even by the chief executive officer (or equivalent).

## Procedural Considerations and Risks

- A ramshackle procurement plan may result in pressures for quick procurement actions, which may lead to the circumventing of fundamental aspects of the procurement cycle (like the need for adequate competition).
- One official should have overall responsibility for the administration of procurement function. Further, the division of responsibilities between the head of the procurement function and the other parts of the organization must be made clear. (The segregation of responsibilities may be set out in documents like internal policies and procedures.)
- The detailed list of anticipated procurement activity should be updated with sufficient frequency for it to remain valid.
- The auditor should assess the implications of any emergency procurement actions. Were such procurement actions the result of genuine, unforeseeable emergencies, or did they arise principally as a result of poor procurement planning?
- The procurement plan's estimated costs (and the timing of projected cash flows) should be reconciled to budgetary and cash flow forecasts on a frequent basis, thereby encouraging the consistency of the procurement plan with the organization's operational needs and liquidity.
- The periodic rotation of procurement employees between procurement actions is a common control to reduce the risks of fraud by discouraging the build-up of long-term relationships (with potentially undesirable consequences) between employees and specific vendors.

## Audit Implications

- An organization that lacks a procurement strategy runs a high risk of having an inconsistent and haphazard procurement process. The auditor should take this into account when auditing procurement.

- The auditor should verify that an organization's procurement plan derives from a procurement strategy that is consistent with the organization's overall objectives.

- The auditor should assess the comprehensiveness of a procurement plan at the level of individual procurement actions.

- The auditor should obtain evidence that an organization updates its procurement plan frequently, and that the plan is periodically reconciled to budgetary and cash flow forecasts.

# CHAPTER 9
# THE REQUEST FOR PROCUREMENT

As noted in the previous chapter, the real beginning of the procurement process may be deemed to start with an organization's overall strategy, planning, and budgeting processes, which establishes the nature and scale of the organization's procurement requirements. In this chapter we shall start to consider individual procurement actions. The chapter is arranged under the following headings:

- The Request for Procurement
- Procedural Considerations and Risks
- Audit Implications

## The Request for Procurement

A procurement function typically receives a "request for procurement" (sometimes known by different terms, like "requisition for procurement"), which is the trigger for the procurement function to initiate the acquisition of a good or service. The request for procurement — and any amendments to it — should be authorized by an appropriate official in accordance with the organization's authorization procedures, and the procurement action should be consistent with the procurement plan (as described in the preceding chapter).

The request for procurement's specifications of the proposed good or service should be sufficiently detailed and should typically include the following:

- Technical specifications for the design and functioning of goods and for the performance of services, and evaluation criteria for both categories. (Where technically appropriate, Bills of Quantities may be attached to the request.)
- Timescales for the procurement function's handling of the request and for delivery of the good or performance of the service.
- Estimated costs (in total and per unit).
- Appropriate accounting information (like general ledger and budget code classifications).
- Environmental, health, and safety considerations.
- Maintenance and spare parts requirements (if appropriate).
- Insurance and warranty information (if appropriate).

Other types of analysis may be attached to the request for procurement, depending on the circumstances. For example, in the case of manufactured goods, a make-or-buy analysis may be attached that summarizes the decision between manufacturing and purchasing an item. Similarly, "rent or buy" or "lease or purchase" analyses may be appropriate for some procurement actions.

The procurement function should evaluate a request for procurement and ask for any additional clarifications and information it feels are needed, both in terms of the technical substance of the request or the administrative requirements placed on the procurement function. In all cases, a request for procurement with weak details and specifications may lead to remedial work later in the procurement process, and it is therefore important to clarify important information early in the procurement cycle.

Requests for procurement should not normally include specific brand names or vendors, to safeguard the competitive element of the procurement process. If it is appropriate to indicate a specific vendor or brand name — where there is a need for compatibility or standardization with existing equipment or services, for example — the request should state "or equivalent" after the name to leave open the door to possible competition.

## Procedural Considerations and Risks

- All procurement actions should have individualized timetables. This may be simply a stated date, or Gantt charts can be used if an envisioned procurement action is sufficiently complex.
- The procurement function should ascertain that sufficient funds are available for individual procurement actions.
- If a proposed procurement action is not listed in the overall procurement plan, or if it is inconsistent with organizational policies in any way, the procurement function should assess the circumstances of the case and obtain suitable authorization before processing the request for procurement.
- Once fulfilled, a request for procurement should be cancelled in the organization's records to reduce the risk of duplicate transactions.
- If a proposed procurement action envisions the possibility of multiple bids by individual vendors (based, for example, on the use of alternative commodities of differing costs), the basis for this should be clearly stated.

## Audit Implications

- The auditor should obtain evidence that individual procurement actions are channelled through requests for procurement, as this is a fundamental internal control over procurement transactions.
- It is important for the auditor to assess whether individual requests for procurement that are selected for review are consistent with the overall procurement plan.

- The auditor should also assess whether individual requests for procurement that are selected for review have sufficient information to allow the procurement function to administer the procurement action effectively and efficiently.
- The auditor should be alert to the avoidance of the use of brand names in requests for procurement so that fair competition is encouraged in the subsequent procurement process.

# CHAPTER 10
# THE IDENTIFICATION OF POTENTIAL VENDORS

After a request for procurement has passed through an organization's established authorization processes, the next stage of the procurement process can begin. The procurement function should establish potential sources for the good or service requested by determining the most appropriate potential vendors. Potential vendors may be identified through a combination of historical dealings with vendors and the participation of new potential vendors.

The selection of potential vendors to participate in a procurement action is a high risk area. Indeed, it is one of the most vulnerable points in the entire procurement process. The exclusion (by error or intent) of a suitable potential vendor can materially affect a procurement process. This chapter is arranged under the following headings:

- The Identification of Potential Vendors
- Finding New Potential Vendors
- Procedural Considerations and Risks
- Audit Implications

## The Identification of Potential Vendors

An organization should maintain a database ("roster" and "portfolio" are also commonly encountered terms) of existing and potential vendors. Existing vendors are those with whom the organization already has a history of transactions. Potential vendors include those who have made unsuccessful offers for specific procurement actions in the past, as well as entirely new potential vendors. The regular infusion of new potential vendors into the procurement process encourages fresh competition and helps to avoid over-reliance on a predefined set of vendors.

Prior to the inclusion of vendors in the vendor database, the procurement function should ensure that the vendors have appropriate technical capabilities for the goods and services they may provide; that they are financially stable[7]; that they comply with any relevant national or international quality and environmental standards; and that they are able to reliably satisfy the organization's procurement demands. As part of the vendor screening process, references may also be sought from the vendors' other customers. In addition, an organization may have a vendor code of conduct, acceptance of which by potential vendors is required, or the organization may require vendors to state their willingness to adhere to its standard terms and conditions. Whatever the precise details of vendor evaluations, consistent criteria should be used.

The procurement function should regularly monitor the vendor database to exclude any vendors who fail to maintain the necessary qualification criteria. Larger organizations may establish vendor review committees to control this important area.

The deletion of a vendor from the database may be appropriate for a wide range of reasons. Examples include poor performance in the supply of goods or services; default on contractual obligations; attempts to bribe the organization's staff members or other serious misconduct; criminal convictions or civil judgments; financial risks; and a consistent refusal to participate in procurement actions.

---

[7]Sources of information that may be used to assess a vendor's financial stability (in terms of liquidity and exposure to debt) include ratio analysis of the vendor's financial statements, and the review of external audit reports and credit ratings.

Readmission to the database may be permitted (for example, on a return to financial health), provided that the basis for the readmission is authorized by a suitable official in the organization and the reasons are fully documented. The organization's procurement function may even assist some vendors in identifying the causes of exclusion and provide guidance on how to make changes to meet the screening requirements. Any such assistance must be available to all vendors on a transparent basis so that the organization does not favor any specific vendors.

## Finding New Potential Vendors

An organization may source new potential vendors through active solicitation. This typically derives from a procurement function's market research to identify the widest possible pool of appropriate potential vendors. Market research may focus on analyses of market activity, existing and emergent technologies, product catalogs, and information that can be obtained from trade organizations and bodies like chambers of commerce. The organization may identify and approach specific vendors through this process.

It should be emphasized that the direct solicitation of potential vendors carries the risks of raising potential vendors' expectations of success in future awards, as well as possible perceptions of organizational favoritism of specific vendors. An invitation to a vendor to participate in a procurement action or to register interest for future procurement actions should in no way imply the success of the vendor in the competitive procurement process. It merely permits vendor participation.

In contrast to the organization directly approaching potential vendors to solicit their interest, another manner of encouraging the participation of suitable, new potential vendors is to create conditions that attract potential vendors to voluntarily approach the organization.

An organization may encourage the invitation of expressions of interest from potential vendors, either for specific procurement actions or on a more general basis. Some organizations (the United Nations, for example) have procurement Web sites through which vendors can register their interest in future procurement activity. Alternatively, advertisements for specific procurement actions can be placed in the media. An international example is given below.

**Millennium Challenge Georgia Fund**
*Reducing Poverty Through Growth*

**Invitation for Bids**

Procurement and Identification No.: ICB No.: SJRRP/CW/04

The Government of Georgia ("Government") and the United States of America, acting through the Millennium Challenge Corporation ("MCC"), executed the Millennium Challenge Account Compact on September 12, 2005 ("Compact"), that sets forth the general terms and conditions on which MCC will provide funding of up to US$295.3 million to the Government for a Millennium Challenge Account program to help facilitate poverty reduction through economic growth in Georgia. The Government, acting through Millennium Challenge Georgia Fund ("MCG"), is responsible for running the program. The Government intends to apply a portion of the proceeds of the MCC Funding (as defined in the Compact) to the Samtskhe-Javakheti Roads Rehabilitation Project ("SJRRP") and to eligible payments under contracts for works to be awarded under International Competitive Bidding ("ICB") No.: ICB/SJRRP/CW/04. This ICB procurement covers six lots:

  1. Lot no. 4.01: Teleti – Partskhisi (included Koda bypass) (27 km)
  2. Lot no. 4.02: Partskhisi – Gokhnari (37.1 km)

3. Lot no. 4.03: Gokhnari – Nardevani (34.6 km)
4. Lot no. 4.04: Nardevani – Satkhe (47.8 km)
5. Lot no. 4.05: Satkhe – Ninotsminda, Akhalkalaki – Armenian Border (50.3 km)
6. Lot no. 4.06: Akhalkalaki – Turkish Border, Akhalkalaki bypass (38.5 km)

We invite you to submit sealed bids for the execution and completion of the contracts covering these lots under the cited ICB.

Bidding will only be open to registered bidders. Bidders must register by completing the **Registration Form** available at www.mcg.ge site and sending it in PDF format to the MCG Procurement Agent's e-mail address: jluneburg@glocoms.com. Registration will be completed when a potential Bidder receives a registration number from the MCG Procurement Agent. Potential bidders may elect on the Registration Form to receive the Bidding Documents and Reference Information Document (RID), (stored electronically on a CD) either (i) in person at the office of the Procurement Agent or (ii) by courier delivery. The cost of such CD and delivery will be borne by MCG.

Potential Bidders also will have an opportunity to inspect a hard copy of the Bidding Documents and the RID at the office of the MCG Procurement Agent.

The RID will include:

- Geotechnical and Materials Report
- Location of state-owned lands along the project roads (Drawings)
- Executive Summary of the Environmental Impact Assessment and Environmental Permit
- Local procedures for temporary land access, quarries, asphalt plant, etc.

Bids submitted by firms that have not registered will not be considered for evaluation and will be returned unopened to the firms.

Registered bidders are invited to submit bids for as many lots as they so choose and for which they are qualified, as described in the Bidding Documents. Bidders should bid separately for each lot for which they elect to prepare a bid. As per the Instructions to Bidders, this procurement may lead to award of one or more contracts. A successful bidder may be awarded a contract for one or for multiple lots, depending on the number of lots for which it qualifies. However, no one bidder may be awarded more than three lots. Bidders are invited to provide a discount in case they will be awarded a contract for multiple lots. Each contract awarded will be a unit rate contract based on a Bill of Quantities. Awards will be subject to the availability of funds.

All bids must be accompanied by a security in the form and amount specified in the Bidding Documents, and must be delivered to the Procurement Agent not later than 6:00 p.m. local Georgian time, on December 27, 2007. Bids will be opened immediately thereafter in the presence of bidders' representatives who choose to attend.

Contact address of the MCG Procurement Agent:

Glocoms Inc.
3rd floor
#9, Nato Vachnadze Street, Tbilisi, Georgia, 0105.
Attention: Jens Luneburg, Team Leader
Tel: +995 (99) 92 31 61
Fax: +995 (32) 92 31 61
E-mail: jluneburg@glocoms.com

Copy to Mr. Giorgi Tvalavadze, MCG Procurement Director
E-mail: g.tvalavadze@mcg.ge

By encouraging expressions of interest from potential vendors, and by subsequently approving them and registering them in the vendor database, the procurement function can expand the organization's pool of potential vendors. In the case of anticipated procurement actions that are expected to be technically complex, the advance screening and approval of vendors for inclusion in the database may be particularly desirable to save time during the procurement action itself.

## Procedural Considerations and Risks

- Over-exposure to one vendor or a small group of vendors presents a risk. The organization should seek to avoid excessive reliance on a small number of vendors.
- The use of standardized vendor registration forms is valuable to encourage a consistent approach to capturing all essential data in a vendor database.
- There should be suitable security and procedural controls over a vendor database, especially in terms of addition to, deletion from, and amendments to the database. Suitable segregations of responsibilities should be established between the procurement and finance functions — a common pattern is for the procurement function to maintain the vendor database while the finance function is responsible for invoice processing and accounts payable routines.
- To ensure that the most appropriate potential vendors compete in the procurement process, the procurement function should take all possible steps to avoid the fraudulent exclusion of suitable vendors and the obstruction of vendors from any source (including other vendors). Any vendor known to have obstructed another vendor should be immediately excluded from the vendor database.

## Audit Implications

- The auditor should assess controls over a database of existing and potential vendors and obtain evidence that the screening of vendors for inclusion in the database is objective, fair, and transparent.
- The auditor should be alert to any signs of favoritism shown to any potential vendors at any stage of a procurement process.
- The auditor should seek evidence of regular management review and monitoring of vendor databases, as this is a crucial process to eliminate unsuitable vendors.

# CHAPTER 11
# COMPETITION

As noted in Part One of this handbook, procurement activity should generally have a transparent and fair competitive foundation to encourage the obtaining of best value for money. This reflects the core economic challenge we discussed in Chapter 3 — how to best use limited resources that have alternative uses. This chapter is arranged under the following headings:

- When Competition is Absent from the Procurement Process
- Quotations and Sealed Bid Tenders
- Auctions
- Vendor Contributions to Defining Technical Specifications
- Procedural Considerations and Risks
- Audit Implications

## When Competition is Absent from the Procurement Process

Good competition tends to encourage good procurement. However, notwithstanding this general principle, there may be justifiable circumstances in which competition may be severely reduced or even eliminated. Exceptions to the need for full competition may include the following:

- The existence of a sole available vendor for a given good or service, or where there is no competitive market. Examples of this include monopolistic conditions; situations in which the supply of a good or service is fixed by legislation or regulatory bodies; and cases where goods or services are patent protected or copyright protected, or subject to intellectual property rights (and there is no suitable substitute available).

- The compatibility of a procured good or service with existing goods and services. For example, an organization may standardize its computer hardware, which involves the use of a specific brand's products and services for a defined period of time.
- An organization may seek a strategic alliance with a specific vendor and negotiate directly with that vendor. Any sole sourcing of a strategic nature should be authorized at the highest levels of the organization.
- The urgency of the need to procure, under genuine emergency conditions, where a delay may involve serious damage or loss to the organization or its employees. Inadequate procurement planning or poor management should not be an excuse for last-minute procurement activity.
- Security reasons, especially for organizations in sensitive sectors like national defense.
- Where objective evaluation is rendered difficult by the nature of the object of the procurement, or where price is not the overriding factor. Such issues are likely to be very rare and may include, for example, the attempt to procure a work of art by a specific artist. Such cases need to be justified and authorized at the highest level of the organization.

To reassure potential vendors, markets, and the wider public, an organization may wish to state (on its official Web site or in an advertisement) the reasons for any major direct, non-competitive contracting with vendors. The auditor is likely to be interested in any material, non-competitive procurement actions.

## Quotations and Sealed Bid Tenders

Where competition is appropriate and feasible, the organization should weigh the costs and benefits of obtaining a suitable level of competitive "intensity" for each procurement action. The extent to which competition is required for procurement actions may be categorized into three scenarios. First, for very small items of expenditure, there may be no need for a formal competitive process, as the administrative costs of arranging for competition may outweigh the benefits. Examples of this type of "spot buying" expenditure include minor purchases typically made from petty cash, when the "intensity" of competition may be restricted to an employee casting an eye over prices displayed on a shop's shelves. Organizations should establish the authority threshold below which competitive procurement is not needed. (This category of minor expenditure is not discussed further in this book.)

The second category concerns acquisitions of goods and services of small to medium value for which competitive quotations are sought. In these cases, in a process sometimes (and aptly) referred to as "shopping," the organization may select and obtain quotations from two or more potential vendors. These will typically be vendors from the database of vendors (established in accordance with the procedures outlined in the previous chapter), but the procurement function's market research may also result in direct approaches to potential vendors not yet registered in its database. Quotations received in this manner do not normally need to have special confidentiality arrangements, as is the case with sealed tender bids.

The third category is that of major procurement items for which a fully competitive process is appropriate, often with sealed tender bids. The organization may undertake strongly competitive procurement actions by asking suitable, potential vendors already listed on the vendor database to tender, or it may undertake an open, public tender process. The latter approach is likely to be most relevant for high-value procurement actions, as the costs of advertising may otherwise be prohibitive in other cases. (The handling of tender bids is discussed further in Chapter 13.) The thresholds at which quotations and tenders are required will depend on the circumstances of the organization.

To ensure a suitable level of competition, there should be an adequate number of potential vendors participating in each procurement action. The procurement function should determine the desired number of participating potential vendors based on the circumstances of each procurement case. For smaller procurement actions, two quotations may be adequate. For larger procurement actions, more than two tender bids are normally appropriate, but too many potential vendors may make the procurement process administratively unwieldy, if not unworkable.

To safeguard the competitive process, at no stage should an organization or its employees give a potential vendor any preferential treatment (for example, "inside" or sensitive information) that might give it an unfair advantage. Therefore, communication with potential vendors should be kept to the minimum needed for a competitive procurement action, and under no circumstances should any communication with a potential vendor compromise the principle of fair competition.

## Auctions

Sealed bid tenders are a common methodology used in procurement actions, not least because of their simplicity and the scope they give for the implementation of strong internal controls. However, other competitive procurement methodologies exist. Dynamic, descending-price auctions may be used, in which potential vendors openly bid against one another to establish the award price. The successful potential vendor is normally the one who offers the lowest auction bid.

The main advantages of auctions[8] are that they promote price visibility and create a setting for intense competition. The auction approach to procurement may be particularly appropriate when an organization is procuring large amounts of a commodity with little technical variation but with potentially significant price volatility. However, major disadvantages of auctions are the necessary logistic arrangements (whether in a physical auction room or through electronic delivery), as well as the risk of collusion among bidders — in an auction, all potential vendors have knowledge of their competitor's prices. In practice, auctions are relatively rare in organizational procurement, and the sealed bid tender process (at least for major procurement actions) is more common. For this reason, this handbook focuses on the sealed bid approach.

## Vendor Contributions to Defining Technical Specifications

Sometimes, the technical specifications of a procurement action are not fully known in advance. This may arise in the cases of highly complex activities and evolving technologies, or when the outputs of a process are not definable in advance. Under these conditions, the procurement function may encourage potential vendors to provide input into the determination of technical requirements. This type of technical negotiation with potential vendors can present significant challenges to the competitiveness of the procurement process.

---

[8]An alternative auction approach is an ascending-price dynamic auction, in which the bidding increases in value from a defined starting point. This is the type of auction typically encountered in selling works of art, or with quickly perishable products like flowers (when it is sometimes known as a "Dutch Auction"), but it is very rare in organizational procurement.

The conduct of procurement actions in the context of technical negotiations is unlikely to be satisfied by one-step, sealed bid tenders, which tend to stifle the necessary technical negotiations between an organization and its potential vendors. An alternative approach is a two-step process, in which the technical evaluation stage is completed before potential vendors are invited to submit their commercial proposals. However, it is often difficult to disentangle the technical and economic aspects of evolving procurement actions, and the auditor should be alert to the risks of this type of procurement action.

## Procedural Considerations and Risks

- The establishment of thresholds at which competitive quotations and tenders are needed is a crucial internal control. There is a risk of either unintentional or deliberate circumvention of thresholds by splitting transactions into smaller parcels of value.
- Any exceptions to the need for competition should be preauthorized by an appropriate official.
- A risk in the process of obtaining quotations or bids is that a vendor may submit offers under various names in order to create an impression of a competitive process. These multiple "offers" merely give an impression of competition but in fact favor an artificially high price, and the procurement function and the auditor should be alert to this risk.
- An organization may establish a minimum "reserve" price above which it will not consider vendor proposals. Depending on the circumstances, the organization may or may not communicate the reserve price to potential vendors.
- If an insufficient number of potential vendors have submitted quotations or bids, the procurement function may approach additional vendors to suggest participation in the procurement

process. For the open tender of major procurement actions, it may advertise (or re-advertise) details of the procurement action to encourage greater participation.

- If any intermediaries are used in the procurement process in order to tap skill sets not available in an organization — for example, the use of real estate consultants to purchase or lease real estate, or the use of brokers to acquire insurance contracts — the competitive principle must be ensured through appropriate organizational oversight of the intermediaries.

- Timescales for procurement actions should be adequate to enable potential vendors to put together their submissions.

- The procurement function should ensure the security and confidentiality of documents it sends to and receives from potential vendors, and address the specific risks of any electronic communications.

- Participation costs may deter potential vendors from submitting bids, particularly in cases where detailed technical submissions are required that are expensive to prepare.

- Sometimes, and particularly for high-value procurement tenders, organizations request from potential vendors a bond or deposit (that is normally returnable). The bond is intended either to encourage the receiving of reliable and serious offers or to safeguard against the risks of future performance default by the successful vendor. The procurement function should set the bond at a fixed sum (for example, $10,000) rather than a percentage of the anticipated cost. This is to avoid giving an indication of the ultimate cost of a procurement action.

## Audit Implications

- The auditor should be alert to ways in which management encourages competition in procurement processes in order to obtain best value for money.
- The auditor should obtain evidence that management respects any thresholds that differentiate competitive intensity in procurement actions (ranging from "spot buying" to "shopping" for quotations to tenders).
- When potential vendors negotiate technical specifications for a procurement action, the procurement process may need to be broken down into discrete stages to make it more manageable. The auditor should review the ways in which management safeguards the competitive elements of such procurement actions.
- Under some circumstances, the scope for competition may be severely reduced or even eliminated. The auditor should obtain evidence to support any significant reductions in procurement competition.

# CHAPTER 12
# TECHNICAL AND ECONOMIC EVALUATIONS

A successful vendor in a procurement process must meet two requirements. First, it must satisfy the technical requirements for the good or service that an organization wishes to procure. Second, it must provide the best value for money of all the technically acceptable offers. Technical and economic evaluations are the means by which the organization reaches decisions on these two crucial elements. This chapter is arranged under the following headings:

- Technical Evaluations
- Economic Evaluations
- Evaluation Hurdles, Combined Evaluation Approaches, and Scores
- Organizations Without Explicit Technical and Economic Evaluations
- Procedural Considerations and Risks
- Audit Implications

## Technical Evaluations

A technical evaluation is an assessment of the specifications of a good or service to be supplied by a potential vendor. It is in an organization's interests to minimize the complexity of technical evaluations as far as possible. However, the technical aspects of a procurement action may range from relatively simple cases to highly complex architectural, engineering, or software specifications that require an expert opinion. The technical evaluation typically consists of reviews of documents submitted by potential vendors in their quotations and bids, but in some cases a procuring organization may decide to directly review (or test samples of) the goods and services themselves.

A cross-functional technical evaluation team, panel, or committee is often established to encourage a full and fair evaluation. In some cases, the organization may seek from external sources expertise that is not available in-house. Examples include engineering consultants, real estate agents, and insurance brokers. In some cases, third parties may be asked to perform the entire technical evaluation under the oversight of the procurement function.

When a procurement function sends out solicitation documents to potential vendors for a procurement action, it is important that the documents include adequate details of technical requirements. This should include the relative importance of alternative technical criteria when applicable. This is to encourage potential vendors to set out clearly comparable quotations and bids, and it also assists in avoiding delays arising from remedial work to correct inadequate proposals. A sufficient level of technical detail in solicitation documents also helps to avoid wasting the time of potential vendors who may be unsuitable. Once a procurement action is underway, any revisions to technical requirements should be communicated to all vendors in the procurement process, and an equal opportunity to resubmit submissions should be given to all potential vendors.

We may take a relatively straightforward case of a cleaning contract for an office to illustrate technical considerations in procurement. A simple, technical starting point for this service is a calculation of the surface area to be cleaned. However, potential vendors need to know matters like the nature of the cleaning surfaces (carpets, tiles, or wooden floors); the required degree of cleaning (often more stringent for medical or scientific premises than for general-purpose offices); the nature of the fixtures and fittings; and the number of staircases.

All of these may affect the cleaning materials and equipment that may be needed, and therefore they are cost-sensitive aspects of the procurement action. This simple example illustrates that even a straightforward procurement topic requires a careful consideration of technical requirements.

Technical evaluations are frequently quantified through a rating or "score" methodology, but in some cases the technical evaluation may be expressed through qualitative assessments. The methodologies suitable to each case should be judged on their merits: there are literally limitless possibilities for technical evaluation methodologies. However, in all circumstances, the technical evaluation should strive for objectivity. Although numerical precision can sometimes be elusive, the use of measurable, quantifiable criteria is desirable.

Examples of technical evaluation criteria are the quality of the proposed good or service; the extent to which a potential vendor has understood the organization's needs; and the potential vendor's commitment to customer service. Where quantifiable criteria are used, it is common for procurement functions to establish a minimum score at which a potential vendor submission is deemed technically acceptable. (Each individual criterion may be weighted for importance in reaching the overall score.)

As noted in the preceding chapter, in cases where technical specifications are difficult to ascertain in advance, the procurement function may request the input of potential vendors in the establishment of technical specifications. This scenario is typically associated with areas of cutting-edge technology or groundbreaking activities, when precise technical specifications cannot be precisely determined at the onset of a procurement process. The auditor should be alert to the risks of situations like this, which may involve a complex series of negotiations with potential vendors. The procurement function should encourage competition and fairness throughout the procurement process by exercising sufficient oversight to protect the integrity of the technical evaluation process.

A situation may arise in which no submissions for a procurement action are technically acceptable. If this happens, the procurement function may either reinitiate the procurement process from the beginning, or ask potential vendors to clarify the technical requirements and thereby refine their proposals. All potential vendors should be given the same opportunity to revise their technical submissions to avoid favoring any of the potential vendors.

## Economic Evaluations

An economic evaluation is an assessment of the best value for money offered by technically acceptable vendor quotations or bids. The procurement function normally performs economic evaluations and limits them to technically acceptable submissions. There is normally no need to evaluate the economic aspects of offers that are not technically compliant. Other than for relatively small offers, two or more individuals should normally perform the economic evaluation to avoid a concentration of duties in one employee's hands.

The economic evaluation should cover matters like the pricing structure of the offer; the proposed cost assumptions; the impact of any offsetting items (like the trade-in of old equipment); and payment terms and the time value of money.[9]

Although the term "commercial evaluation" is often used, we use the term "economic evaluation" on the grounds that the evaluation

---

[9]The "time value of money" refers to the impact of interest rates, inflation, and general economic risks. All things being equal, a dollar paid now is worth more than a dollar paid in the future.

should consider all relevant costs, not merely the prices quoted by potential vendors. As noted in Chapter 4, the procurement function should consider all the incremental costs that would arise from a decision to proceed with a specific vendor for a procurement action. Examples of costs that may not be stated in a potential vendor's submission but which may nonetheless be real costs to the organization if it proceeds with a given procurement action include training costs for employees unfamiliar with a new product or service; maintenance and spare parts; the ultimate disposal costs for assets; and environmental costs.

Some costs (like reputation costs) are difficult to quantify, but they should nonetheless be evaluated. Any contingent costs should be assessed on the most appropriate basis. For example, costs and discounts may be linked to activity levels, or they may be subject to market fluctuations (in the case of commodity prices).

If all the potential vendors' submissions exceed a reserve price or other defined threshold of authorized costs, additional authorizations at a suitable level of the organization are needed. Alternatively, the organization may decide to re-solicit submissions or contact all potential vendors to give them an equal and fair opportunity to revise their costs downwards. No "bidding wars" should be permitted (unless it is organizational policy to undertake auctions), and in the revision of submissions all potential vendors must be offered the same opportunity to resubmit their bids.

## Evaluation Hurdles, Combined Evaluation Approaches, and Scores

The procurement function should permit only the submissions from potential vendors that pass the hurdle of technical acceptability to proceed to the economic evaluation. This is intuitive and based on common sense — there is little point in procuring a good or service that is not technically acceptable. Under this hurdle approach, the selection of the supplier is normally made on the basis of the lowest technically acceptable quotation or bid.

The search for the lowest costs may be tempered by non-economic considerations, like the availability of vendor support and advice for an ongoing service. We may consider this through an example of a procurement process in which three potential vendors have complied with the technical specifications for the installation of computer hardware in the clerical offices of a large organization. Although the three vendors have provided almost indistinguishable computer hardware, there are significant differences in their approach to customer service, in delivery schedules, and in warranties. These latter aspects have added or detracted significant value to or from their submissions, and the procuring organization undertakes an economic evaluation that takes account of these factors alongside the vendors' proposed selling prices.

In cases of perceived gradations of technical acceptability, some organizations rank potential vendors by using a system of weighted scores that intermingle technical and economic aspects. There is a wide variation of scoring methodologies, the details of which need not concern us in this handbook.[10] Scores may be weighted between the technical and economic evaluations, as well as among individual criteria within the technical and economic evaluations.

Combined evaluation approaches of this nature reflect the core economic challenge of procurement that we discussed in Chapter 3 —

---

[10]A series of scoring methodologies — lowest bid, highest bid, average, linear, and parabolic — are discussed in Nicola Dimitri, Gustavo Piga, and Giancarlo Spagnolo (ed.) *Handbook of Procurement* (Cambridge, UK: Cambridge University Press, revised edition, 2006), 304-310.

how to achieve the best use of limited resources that have alternative uses. A procurement function should deploy the most suitable methodology for the circumstances of individual procurement actions. For example, an organization that is indifferent to the relative importance of the technical and economic aspects of a procurement process may allocate scores between the two evaluations on a 50/50 basis. An organization that wishes to stress quality over cost for a procurement action may give a weighting of 70% to the technical evaluation and 30% to the economic evaluation. In contrast, an organization that wishes to stress cost over quality may choose a weighting of 30% to the technical evaluation and 70% to the economic evaluation. The auditor should be aware of the ways in which scoring methods can influence the outcome of a procurement action, and how the sensitivity of scoring methodologies may be open to manipulation.

It should be noted that even in the case of a combined evaluation approach, the technical evaluation should be completed before the combined approach is started in order to eliminate any technically unacceptable submissions.

## Organizations Without Explicit Technical and Economic Evaluations

Some organizations have a sole evaluation process that collapses the distinction between technical and economic evaluations. In practice, a cursory review tends to substitute the technical evaluation, and the economic evaluation becomes the core of the process. This approach may be justified for very small organizations, for those with extremely simple operations, or for those who undertake technically simple procurement actions. However, in general, the distinction between economic and technical evaluations is a valuable and essential one that decreases the risks of suboptimal procurement activity.

## Procedural Considerations and Risks

- A procurement function should ensure that the technical terms of reference of a procurement action are clearly communicated to all potential vendors.
- Technical and economic evaluations must be properly documented and recorded.
- All evaluation reports should be authorized by an appropriate official of the organization.
- When potential vendors contribute to determining precise technical specifications, there may be a heightened risk of collusion between organizational employees and potential vendors to "fix" the technical aspects so as to give an unfair advantage to a specific potential vendor.
- In cases where potential vendors are permitted to modify either the technical or economic aspects of their submissions, the same modification opportunities must be given to all potential vendors. No potential vendors should be placed at a disadvantage in the procurement process, and impartiality should underpin all communications with potential vendors.
- All evaluations and scoring systems should be transparent, impartial, and fair.
- Standardized templates for vendor submission documents can be useful to ensure the completeness, consistency, and comparability of information in procurement actions, but templates should be flexible enough to cope with the additional information that may be needed for complex procurement actions.
- It is necessary for a procurement function to communicate to potential vendors the required method of delivery of their technical and economic offers to ensure compliance

with organizational requirements. If appropriate, potential vendors should be instructed to seal separately the technical and economic submissions to permit the organization to review the former before the latter.

- A potential vendor's economic submission may state abnormally low prices. Very low costs may be legitimate if a potential vendor is anxious to break into a new market or expand market share at low profit (or at break-even level, or even at a loss). Potential vendors with excess capacity or inventory may also submit offers with abnormally low costs. The procurement function should use prudent judgment in assessing best value for money in such a situation. Abnormally low proposed costs may not be sustainable and may affect the quality of the good or service acquired in the longer term, as a vendor may seek to cut quality to save costs.

- The distortion of technical and economic evaluation scores is a major risk in procurement processes.

## Audit Implications

- The auditor should review the integrity, impartiality, and accuracy of technical and economic evaluations undertaken in relation to procurement actions.

- For economic evaluations, the auditor should obtain evidence that the procuring organization evaluates the total, incremental costs attributable to a proposed procurement action.

- The auditor should understand and review for reasonableness any "scoring" methodologies used for technical and economic evaluations.

- The auditor should ensure that the selection of vendors follows logically from the results of the technical and economic evaluations.

# CHAPTER 13
# SELECTION OF THE
# PREFERRED VENDOR AND
# AWARD OF CONTRACT

This chapter considers the procedures and internal controls surrounding the selection of vendors for the award of contracts for procurement actions. This is a highly sensitive stage of the procurement process, which can be undermined by careless administration or deliberate fraud. This chapter is arranged under the following headings:

- The Handling of Submissions from Potential Vendors
- Selection of the Preferred Vendor
- Notifications to Unsuccessful Potential Vendors
- Award of Contract
- Procedural Considerations and Risks
- Audit Implications

## The Handling of Submissions from Potential Vendors

In the process of selecting a preferred vendor for a procurement action, the procurement function should receive and handle potential vendors' offers in a rigorous, confidential, and transparent manner that ensures the equal treatment of all potential vendors. For quotations, there may be no particular confidentiality requirements (other than those for the normal handling of operational documentation with sensitive information). In the case of tender bids, it is customary for potential vendors to submit sealed bids, and for the organization to hold the sealed bids in custody until they are formally opened. For reasons of segregation of responsibilities, a procurement function usually does not have custody of sealed bids — the finance or legal functions may hold them instead. A secure location for unopened bids is essential, and most organizations tend to use locked safes.

An organizational panel or committee established for the purpose of tender bid opening frequently oversees the unsealing and recording of the bids at a defined time and at a stipulated location. This practice is intended to ensure the transparency and rigor of the process by reducing the possibilities of interference with the sealed bids. As bids are opened, it is customary for them to be read aloud and immediately recorded.

A committee or panel of this nature may consist of representatives from a variety of organizational functions to ensure the inclusion of employees not directly connected to the procurement action. For major procurement actions, an organization may also permit potential vendors to observe the opening of bids, but the participation of potential vendors should normally be restricted to that of silent observers. For procurement actions that have a significant public interest, representatives of other institutions (like trade associations and government officials) may also observe the opening of tenders. Sometimes, even members of the public may be permitted to attend a tender opening that is deemed to be in the public interest. In all cases, irrespective of the planned attendance at the event, the organization should give adequate notice to interested parties of the time and place of the opening of the sealed bids.

It is relatively straightforward for an organization to receive and hold in custody sealed, hardcopy bids from potential vendors. Additional controls are needed to administer submissions received by fax or by electronic means. Dedicated fax machines and e-mail addresses with strictly restricted access are the minimum requirements, but for many organizations the risks surrounding submissions of this type appear to be too high. This may explain the continuing widespread practice of requesting hardcopy bid submissions from potential vendors.

The procurement function should make formal records of all bid offers and mark any original submission documentation from potential vendors by stamping, signing, or perforating documents. This is to ensure that subsequent documentation may not be added to (or replace) the original submission. Additionally, the procurement function should record any non-submissions of potential vendors that it had contacted at the solicitation stage.

The procurement function should set out clear timescales in the solicitation documents it sends to potential vendors, and should exclude late submissions from the procurement process. However, the procurement function may allow exceptions to this. For example, a late submission caused by a postal delay may be accepted when it is clear from the postmark that the submission had been posted in what would normally have been sufficient time. An appropriate official in the organization should authorize any such exceptions to submission deadlines.

The modification of quotation or bid submissions should only be permitted for clearly definable and appropriate reasons — examples include the correction of calculation errors (like mistakes in units of measure that would be misleading, or the inaccurate totalling of numbers) and the correction of technical errors (like the physical dimensions of an asset). If a procurement function allows one potential vendor to modify its quotation or bid, it must also offer the same opportunity to all the potential vendors to ensure impartiality.

## Selection of the Preferred Vendor

Following the technical and economic evaluations (discussed in the preceding chapter), the procurement function identifies the preferred vendor as the one whose offer conforms to technical requirements and gives the best value for money. The procurement function normally formalizes this process by summarizing and presenting the finds of the technical and economic evaluations to a suitable authority in the organization.

Some organizations — for example, in the United Nations system — have committees that review procurement proposals over a given threshold. A committee of this nature is usually comprised of a range of interested parties in the organization, including participants from the legal and finance functions. The organization should provide committee members with sufficient information to assess the proposed selection of the preferred vendor — at a minimum, an overview of the procurement action, the number of potential vendors who participated, and comparative summaries of technical and economic evaluations. The committee's meetings should be minuted.

A procurement proposal committee should meet face-to-face as far as possible to encourage debate of the issues at stake. This is preferable to a reliance on impersonal communication channels or "silent procedures" whereby documents are circulated and committee members' comments are solicited. As its name suggests, under a "silent procedure" silence is taken to be agreement with the proposed selection of a preferred vendor. The obvious risk here is that silence might not amount to agreement, as an individual may not see the proposal if absent from the office, or if the internal documentation distribution system fails.

If a procurement process results in a very small number of potential vendors that pass the technical evaluation — two, perhaps, or even one — the procurement function should undertake additional procedures to ensure that the costs in the technically acceptable offers give best value for money. These alternative procedures normally focus on assessments of the reasonableness of proposed costs in relation to existing market rates and trade and industry norms. The procurement function must exercise prudence under such circumstances, as the organization tends to encounter higher risks in the absence of strong competition.

If no submissions from potential vendors meet the required technical and economic criteria, an appropriate official should authorize a repeat or modification of the solicitation process, or the end of the procurement action. If the lack of success of the procurement action was attributable to a lack of competition, the procurement function should consider wider advertising of the procurement action.

The procurement function should take seriously any objections or protests received from unsuccessful vendors, or indeed from any potential vendor, at any stage of the procurement action. Without unduly delaying the procurement process, the procurement function should make an assessment of the objections, and the extent to which the objections present a risk to the integrity of the procurement action and even to the organization as a whole. The procurement function should establish a procedure to handle objections of this nature, and for segregation of responsibilities the evaluation of objections should involve an employee or organizational function not directly involved or implicated in the objection.

The organization should act on any legitimate objections after the due process is followed. In serious cases (like evidence of collusion between potential vendors) it may be necessary to restart the procurement action. If a credible objection is made after an award is made, the award may need to be suspended until the matter is resolved.

## Notifications to Unsuccessful Potential Vendors

Out of courtesy, and after the selection of the preferred vendor is completed, the procurement function should normally notify unsuccessful potential vendors of the outcome of the procurement process. Generally, information divulged to unsuccessful vendors should be modest in scope. It is common to provide the name of the successful vendor; the ranking of the unsuccessful vendor out of the total number of submissions received; possibly the value at which the award was made; and (as far as this is in accordance with the organization's confidentiality and privacy requirements) the reasons for the lack of success of the unsuccessful participants, based on the technical or economic evaluations. The procurement function may also make some of this information publicly available for large procurement actions (through an organizational Web site, for example), but while transparency is generally desirable the organization should also respect the privacy of unsuccessful potential vendors.

For large procurement actions, a procurement function may debrief unsuccessful vendors in face-to-face meetings on the reasons for their lack of success. The procurement function should normally limit any such debriefings to the technical evaluations of the potential vendors' own submissions so that potential vendors can identify weaknesses that can be remedied in future submissions. Under no circumstances should submissions of rival potential vendors be divulged, from the perspective of either the technical or economic evaluations. For this reason, the procurement function should avoid any comparative analysis of submissions in its discussions with the participants in a concluded procurement action.

## Award of Contract

In our definition of procurement in Chapter 1, we emphasized the legal aspects of procurement activity by referring to the acquisition of goods and services "through contractual agreement."[11] On the successful conclusion of the technical and economic evaluation processes and the selection of the preferred vendor, the organization notifies the vendor and prepares a formal contract. A contract is referred to here as a legally enforceable agreement between an organization and a vendor that sets out the terms and conditions for the supply of goods or services.

Contractual agreements are essential to fix responsibilities and rights in procurement, and to offer some protection to both parties from unexpected events. The stability offered by contracts with vendors promotes efficient and effective organizational activity. All contracts should be in writing and adhere to any legal execution requirements of the jurisdictions that the agreement is intended to cover. This is an area of major risk for organizations with international activities. For example, any notarization of contracts applicable to specific jurisdictions must be followed.

Contractual negotiations with vendors should involve the procurement function and relevant operational employees, in addition to the legal function. Cross-functional input into a contract's text may assist in reducing risks and costs through the contribution of a balanced and comprehensive mix of skills and knowledge.

---

[11]It is beyond the scope of this handbook to go into the details of contract law. Only brief outlines of key considerations, risks, and controls are possible here.

The complexity of a contract will tend to mirror the complexity of the underlying procurement action. In straightforward cases, contracts may take the form of purchase orders, which are simplified agreements that list goods and services and set out the organization's standard terms and conditions for procurement. In such cases, the use of a standard template minimizes the risks of inappropriate contractual terms. (Contracts may not be needed for very low value acquisitions of goods and services; the organization must decide on an appropriate threshold for the requirement for a contract.) In more complex cases, the contract may need to be tailored to specific circumstances. Contract law is rich with disputes between contracting parties. In all cases, the legal agreement should use language that is as unambiguous as possible.

The typical basic contents of agreements include the following:

- Details of the parties to the agreement.
- The jurisdiction of the agreement (of particular importance for international agreements).
- A precise description of the goods or services to be supplied.
- A definition of the period of time covered by the agreement, and important milestones within the overall contractual period.
- Clear statements of the rights and obligations of both parties, including any appropriate record-keeping requirements.
- References to the applicability of the organization's standard terms and conditions, with details of any deviations or special conditions.
- Payment details. The timing of payments should either be linked to clearly defined deliverables, or if the basis is one of time only, the payment dates should be clearly stated.
- Any applicable warranty, guarantee, and insurance arrangements.

- Provisions for damages, remedies, and compensation in the cases of the non-delivery of goods; the non-performance of services; inadequacies in quality; cost overruns; and any other material breach of contract.
- Procedures for the handling of disputes, including dispute resolution arrangements like third-party mediation, arbitration, and civil action in the courts.
- Any important taxation implications of the contract (especially for international agreements).
- Procedures for any future amendment of the contract.
- Details of the termination of the agreement after all contractual obligations have been met.

Additional elements for inclusion in the contract may include any unusual patterns of delivery of goods or performance of services. Examples are the "calling off" or "drawing down" of goods in unpredictable patterns, and the trade-in of old equipment against the cost of newly acquired items.

Although cross-functional input into the preparation of a contract may be important, the legal function should review the contract for compliance with all appropriate legal requirements prior to its signing. The same applies for any amendments to the contract.

Copies of the contract should be made available to those who later evaluate the delivery of the good or performance of the service, if the contractual details are necessary to support such an evaluation. (This topic is discussed further in the following chapter.)

The contract should be fixed for a suitable duration. The organization should avoid being locked into long-term contracts from which extrication may be desirable but difficult, while simultaneously avoiding a situation in which an important vendor can legally walk away from a contractual agreement and plunge the organization into operational trouble. Longer-term contracts may be appropriate for requirements of a continuing nature, for projects that span several years, and when long lead times are needed for the delivery of goods.

The renewal or non-renewal of contracts can be an effective means of rewarding or punishing vendors for their performance. However, the frequent rewarding of good vendors should not override the periodic need for competition. The re-tendering of contracts should be done periodically.

## Procedural Considerations and Risks

- To ensure the confidentiality and safe arrival of sealed, hardcopy tender bid submissions, a procurement function might stipulate that courier services or registered mail should be used. If an organization chooses to accept faxed or electronic submissions, very strong controls must be in place to maintain the security and confidentiality of the submissions.
- The safe custody of sealed bids prior to their opening is an important internal control. A member of a committee or panel for opening bids who notes any irregularities should immediately report it to the other members of the committee and, as appropriate, to a suitable official in the organization.
- The procurement function should record any withdrawal of offers by potential vendors and obtain in writing the potential vendor's withdrawal decision. After ascertaining the reason for the withdrawal, the procurement function should assess what (if any) action the organization should take. For example, if a potential vendor withdraws amid allegations

of collusion among other vendors, this may have serious implications for the validity of a procurement action.

- If an internal auditor attends a committee meeting for opening sealed bids, or a meeting to assess procurement actions, he or she should participate as a non-voting observer to ensure independence from managerial decision-making.
- Verbal agreements with vendors should be avoided in favor of written agreements.
- Contractual agreements with vendors should be signed by authorized signatories representing both parties. For the procuring organization, a suitable official should award and sign the contract before any legally binding commitment is made. This is to avoid a situation of a *fait accompli*, in which a legally binding commitment is made before a formal agreement is in place.
- An organization should have sanctions for employees who enter into unauthorized procurement contracts. Employees may even be held personally liable for such unauthorized actions.
- Standard terms and conditions generally minimize risks. Amendments to standard terms and conditions should be authorized by a suitable official in an organization on the basis of an evaluation of the potential risks of any such amendments.
- If any Electronic Data Interchange element is present in a procurement action, the opinion of the organization's information services function should be sought on the technical capability of the organization to meet its obligations.
- Some agreements with vendors include a provision for an organization to audit the performance of the vendor's contractual obligations. This is common for large procurement actions, and it may be a vital internal control.

## Audit Implications

- The auditor should look for evidence that a procurement function receives and administers submissions from potential vendors in a consistent and impartial manner.
- The auditor should assess the adequacy of the security of sealed bid tender documentation.
- The auditor should review the manner in which a procurement function evaluates any credible complaints received in relation to the propriety of procurement actions.
- The auditor should obtain evidence that appropriate legal agreements underpin an organization's relations with its vendors.

# CHAPTER 14
# THE RECEIPT AND EVALUATION OF GOODS AND SERVICES

An organization should adequately monitor and evaluate the goods and services it procures. This monitoring of deliverables is crucial to ensure that vendors and the organization meet the rights and obligations set out in contractual agreements. In this way, the evaluation of procured goods and services is intended to contribute to the achievement of the goals of procurement actions.[12] This chapter is arranged under the following headings:

- The Receipt of Goods and Services
- Record Keeping
- Procedural Considerations and Risks
- Audit Implications

## The Receipt of Goods and Services

For every awarded procurement action, an appropriate official should ensure that the organization has received goods and services in accordance with the terms and conditions of the relevant contract.

---

[12]Sometimes a distinction is made between the monitoring of vendor performance during a contract and the subsequent evaluation of the vendor's performance after a contractual agreement has ended. This book does not make this distinction, but instead uses the term "monitoring" to refer to the accumulation of information relating to vendor performance, and "evaluation" to refer to the assessment of the quality of vendor performance.

The process of "receiving" goods and services covers not only the existence of the good or service, but also an evaluation of its quality and of the extent to which it conforms to agreed deliverables.

Methods to monitor and evaluate procured, tangible goods include steps like physical inspection, counting, and perhaps also sampling for quality testing. Counting is a basic but valuable methodology, as the shipping short of agreed quantities is a classic type of fraudulent or negligent activity associated with procurement. Methods to monitor and evaluate services include observation, the use of metrics that measure performance (like error rates and user satisfaction), and benchmarking with procurement activities outside the organization (when information of this nature is available).

In all cases, the quality, cost, and timeliness of the delivery of goods or the performance of services are likely to be pertinent. Appropriate information on the quality of goods and services must be defined, captured, and evaluated consistently. The criteria and standards for the evaluation of goods and services must be clear and unambiguous, even when judgment is needed. Where appropriate, copies of the contractual agreement with a vendor should be made available to those who evaluate the delivery of a good or service, if the contractual details are necessary to support the evaluation.

The receipt of a vendor invoice or a request for payment often triggers the procurement-related receiving process. This allows for both a verification of the accuracy of the expenditure and an evaluation of the quality of the good or service procured. The authorization of the invoice ties into accounts payable routines that are beyond the scope of this handbook, but it should be recognized that the authorization of receipt of a good or service can be central to internal controls in areas like disbursements, accounts payable, and the general ledger.

An invoice-triggered evaluation of a good or service may be entirely independent of ongoing vendor contract monitoring procedures, though there may be a meaningful overlap between the two. An example can illustrate the difference between ongoing monitoring and specific, invoice-triggered receiving actions. If one considers the case of an organization that has a contractual relationship with a provider of office cleaning services, the organization should monitor and evaluate the performance of this service on an ongoing basis in order to ensure adequate performance of the service. This may involve periodic inspection of the quality of the cleaning service and a record of complaints received about the service. In addition to this ongoing process of evaluation, the receipt of an invoice from the vendor triggers the procurement receiving process, which requires an official to formally confirm adequate "receipt" of the service. The official may take into account the results of the ongoing monitoring, but he or she may also undertake additional evaluation steps to justify payment of the vendor invoice. Ongoing monitoring is especially important in relation to longer-term projects where billing may be infrequent.

An organization should formally designate the officials who are authorized to receive goods and services. In all cases, a receiving official should have sufficient knowledge and experience to inspect, evaluate, and make judgments on the receipt of a good or service. To ensure a suitable segregation of responsibilities, receiving officials should be unable to receive and evaluate goods or services for which they can amend procurement, legal, or accounting records.

## Record Keeping

The manner in which goods and services are recorded as received and evaluated should be of major concern to an organization. In small or informal organizations, the receiving process may be documented only on an exceptional basis when problems occur, but this approach is unlikely to offer adequate internal controls for larger organizations. An organization may prepare formal receiving reports, in which a narrative description of the receipt of the good or service is given, signed (with dates) by the receiving officials. A receiving report may be in either hardcopy or electronic format.

The use of receiving reports may be tied to cost thresholds at the level of either the individual invoice or, better, for the cost of the procurement action as a whole. Detailed accounts payable procedures are beyond the scope of this handbook, but it is sufficient to note the importance of recording the acceptable receipt of goods and services prior to the payment of related vendor invoices.

An alternative to the use of receiving reports is the use of ink stamps on vendor invoices, which set out spaces for receiving officials to sign and make notes to indicate receipt. This is unlikely to be satisfactory for complex procurement actions, as receiving reports should allow for any appropriate, expansive narrative explanations of the results of the receiving and evaluation process. Whatever the manner in which the receiving process is recorded, any deficiencies or irregularities in the receipt of a good or service should be recorded and reported to an appropriate official for action.

## Procedural Considerations and Risks

- Receiving officials should have sufficient knowledge and experience — and sufficient information — to evaluate the good or service they are responsible for receiving.
- Formal inspection schedules and timetables may be appropriate to guide receiving officials in the performance of their duties.

- The rejection of goods and services that do not conform to agreed standards is essential for an evaluation process to be effective.
- The receiving process must capture and evaluate any corrective actions.
- Feedback mechanisms with vendors should be established to allow for any timely corrective action for variances between expected and actual deliverables.
- Vendors may be involved in more than one procurement action. For an overall vendor performance evaluation, the organization needs to consolidate and evaluate all the procurement actions that relate to a specific vendor.
- In technically complex cases, it may be necessary to use an outside consultant to evaluate a good or service. Where appropriate, this should be specified in the contractual agreement with the vendor.

## Audit Implications

- The auditor should assess the extent to which an organization adequately monitors and evaluates the goods and services it procures.
- It is important that the auditor reviews the adherence of evaluation criteria for vendor performance to both contractually agreed terms and sensible, relevant performance measures.
- The auditor should obtain evidence of the appropriateness of an organization's segregation of responsibilities between its receiving function and related transaction processing.
- The auditor should be alert to the linkages between an organization's payment of vendor invoices and the acceptable receipt of the underlying goods or services.

# PART THREE
# CONCLUSIONS

# CHAPTER 15
# CONCLUDING THOUGHTS

We have suggested in this handbook that the fundamentals of procurement are relatively straightforward. In contrast, the details of how to administer procurement processes may be highly complex in organizations that have established rigorous procurement policies and practices. The procurement manuals of some organizations resemble telephone directories in size — sometimes even a shelf of telephone directories. The volume of information involved in procurement activity is often immense, and it is advisable for the auditor to stand back now and then from all this detail to discern the sinews of core principles among the technicalities (and trivia) of a busy procurement function.

The complexity of procurement can be reduced to a relatively small number of core principles. High among these principles is the foundation of procurement on a basic economic challenge, which is the search for best value for money in the acquisition of goods and services. From this core principle flow the main considerations of procurement — the use of competition to encourage downward pressures on vendor prices; the correct identification of the costs and benefits of procurement proposals; appropriate technical and economic evaluations of vendor proposals; a commitment to a fair, ethical, and transparent procurement process; and a suitable recognition of the importance of socioeconomic factors. It is the author's view that this economic conceptual architecture facilitates the auditing of procurement.

There is much at stake in the field of procurement, including the financial success of organizations. It is an area to which the auditor can bring a significant amount of sound advice.

# CHAPTER 16
# SOURCES OF
# FURTHER INFORMATION[13]

## Published Sources

Nicola Dimitri, Gustavo Piga, and Giancarlo Spagnolo (editors), *Handbook of Procurement* (Cambridge, UK: Cambridge University Press, revised edition, 2006).

> This is a valuable collection of essays on various aspects of the procurement process. Academic in tone, yet also providing practical information, this book's exhaustive analysis of procurement is likely to be of most interest to auditors who undertake a significant proportion of their work in the area of procurement. At more than 500 pages, it is probably a little too heavy for the occasional auditor of procurement. It does not address audit concerns directly, but it provides significant background information on procurement best practices.

Fred Sollish and John Semanik (editors), *The Procurement and Supply Manager's Desk Reference* (Hoboken, NJ: Wiley, 2007).

> While more practical in orientation than the previous book, this is also is a large volume that is most likely to be of interest to auditors who undertake a significant amount

---

[13]This chapter includes references to Web-based resources. Please note that the persistence or accuracy of Internet-based resources may be subject to change.

of work in the area of procurement. As with the previous book, it does not address audit concerns directly, but does contain excellent, general information on best practices and innovation in procurement.

David McNamee, *Auditing Purchasing and Contracts* (Alamo, CA: Pleier Corporation, 2004).

This is an introductory-level workbook, in CD-ROM format, that covers various aspects of procurement. It offers valuable materials for experienced auditors as well as for novices. McNamee has prepared this material specifically with the auditor in mind. The workbook includes topics like fraud risk management and procurement benchmarking.

"Research Report on Audits of Procurement," Exhibit 21-8 in Lawrence B. Sawyer, Mortimer A. Dittenhofer, and James H. Scheiner (editors) *Sawyer's Internal Auditor* (Altamonte Springs, FL: The Institute of Internal Auditors, 5th edition, 2003), 905-909.

This exhibit, in one of the foundation texts for internal auditing, offers a brief but useful summary of major procurement risks.

United Nations, *Report of the Office of Internal Oversight Services on the Audit of the Application of the Best Value for Money Principle in United Nations Procurement* (A/61/846, dated 10 April 2007, available from www.un.org/depts/oios).

Although this is an organization-specific audit report, it is in the public domain and touches on procurement themes that have a wide resonance. It deals with defining and applying the concept of best value for money; the effectiveness of competition in the procurement process; and the methodologies used to select vendors.

## Institutional Resources

Institute for Supply Management (available from: www.ism.ws) The Chartered Institute of Purchasing and Supply (available from: www.cpis.org)

These two professional organizations, based respectively in the United States and the United Kingdom, have a range of procurement-related materials and guidance. Materials on these Web sites are likely to be of most interest to auditors who undertake a significant proportion of their work in the area of procurement, as they address many specialist areas.

Incoterms (available from: www.iccwbo.org/incoterms)

Incoterms are standard trade definitions, intended for international contracts, which have been developed by the International Chamber of Commerce. Incoterms have been endorsed by the United Nations Commission on International Trade Law (UNCITRAL).

Organization for Economic Co-operation and Development (OECD) (available from: www.oecd.org)

A Paris-based international organization, the OECD has published extensively on procurement topics like bribery and environmental considerations. The OECD Web site has details of its publications.

The United Nations Global Compact (available from:
www.unglobalcompact.org)

The UN Global Compact offers an international framework
for corporate citizenship in the areas of human rights,
anticorruption, and sustainability.  It sets out principles for
organizations to adopt on a voluntary basis.

# GLOSSARY

In this handbook, we generally avoided the use of acronyms, but for reference purposes, some common acronyms are given below.

Bid — An offer by a potential vendor, in the context of a tender, to supply a good or service at a stated price.

Bill of Materials (BOM) — An alternative name for Bill of Quantities, common in the United Kingdom and other countries with a strong British influence.

Bill of Quantities (BOQ) — A summary of the raw materials and other elements of a manufactured good or asset.

Commercial Evaluation (CE) — An alternative term for "economic evaluation."

Economic Evaluation (EE) — An assessment of the best value for money given by technically acceptable vendor offers.

e-Procurement — Electronic procurement, i.e., procurement conducted through information and networking technologies like the Internet and electronic data interchange systems.

e-Tendering — Electronic tendering (see the entry "tender").

Good — A tangible product, merchandise, or commodity (for example, a desk or a security fence).

Invitation to Quote (ITQ) — An alternative term for "request for quotation."

Invitation to Tender (ITT) — An alternative term for "request for tender."

Offer — A proposal by a potential vendor, in the form of either a quotation or a bid, to supply a good or service with defined technical specifications at a stated price.

Procurement — The obtaining, through contractual agreement, of the timely and correct delivery of goods and services at best value for money.

Quotation — An offer by a potential vendor to supply a good or service at a stated price.

Request for Procurement (RFP) — A request originating from within an organization, addressed to its procurement function, for the acquisition of a good or service.

Request for Quotation (RFQ) — An invitation to a potential vendor to make a quotation for a procurement action.

Request for Tender (RFT) — An invitation to a potential vendor to participate in a tender for a procurement action.

Requisition for Procurement (RFP) — An alternative term for "request for procurement."

Reserve Price — The maximum vendor price that an organization is willing to accept for a procurement action.

Service — An economic activity that relies on labor rather than on tangible goods (for example, cleaning services, security patrols).

Solicitation — An invitation to a potential vendor to submit an offer to supply a good or a service.

Technical Evaluation (TE) — An assessment of the specifications of a good or service to be provided by a potential vendor.

Tender — A competitive bidding process in which potential vendors submit technical details and the prices at which they are willing to offer a good or service.